CONCEPTUAL MODELS in TEACHER EDUCATION

An Approach To Teaching and Learning

by

JOHN R. VERDUIN, JR.
Associate Professor of Education
State University of New York
College at Geneseo

The American Association of Colleges
for Teacher Education
1201 Sixteenth Street, N. W.
Washington, D. C. 20036

THE AMERICAN ASSOCIATION OF COLLEGES FOR TEACHER EDUCATION
1201 Sixteenth Street, N.W., Washington, D. C. 20036
Library of Congress Catalog Card Number: 67-17075
Printed in the U.S.A.

Additional copies of this publication are available at $3.00 per copy.
Order from:

DR. EDWARD C. POMEROY, *Executive Secretary*
The American Association of Colleges for Teacher Education
1201 Sixteenth Street, N.W., Washington, D. C. 20036

SECOND PRINTING, OCTOBER 1968

Foreword

The American Association of Colleges for Teacher Education, in cooperation with Associated Organizations for Teacher Education (AOTE), contracted with the United States Office of Education (Educational Media Branch) for a twenty-seven month program entitled "A Project to Improve the Professional Sequence in Preservice Teacher Education through the Selective and Planned Use of New Media." One of the results of the TEAM Project (Teacher Education and Media) was the publication and wide distribution by the AACTE of *A Proposal for the Revision of the Pre-service Professional Component of a Program of Teacher Education*. This publication stimulated a great deal of interest on the part of teacher educators in the field.

Under the leadership of John R. Verduin, Jr., the Division of Education of the State University College, Geneseo, New York, using the TEAM proposal as a guide, engaged in an academic year study of the theoretical foundations of teacher education. A series of faculty seminars was held throughout the school year, and leading educational researchers and theoreticians were called in to serve as resource persons. These seminars served to upgrade and stimulate the teacher education faculty and provided an instrument for approaching the teacher education curriculum in a more analytical manner. This present book contains an edited version of the presentations and discussions engaged in by the faculty, and it is hoped that others involved in teacher preparation programs will find stimulation in these materials.

The New York State Department of Education deserves special recognition for supporting this effort. Commendation is also due the college administration for its continuing encouragement to Dr. Verduin and his staff. The Association also wishes to thank Dr. Verduin for making this manuscript available. While the opinions concerning the preparation of teachers expressed herein are those of Dr. Verduin and the special resource people, they are sure to stimulate considerable discussion in the field. The Association commends this effort to seek new and innovative approaches to teacher preparation.

A special note of appreciation is given to Mrs. Rebecca Fiske for her work in translating the original manuscript into book form.

WALTER J. MARS
Associate Secretary

March 1967

Acknowledgments

Edmund J. Amidon and Ned Flanders. THE ROLE OF THE TEACHER IN THE CLASSROOM: A MANUAL FOR UNDERSTANDING AND IMPROVING TEACHERS' CLASSROOM BEHAVIOR. Minneapolis: Paul S. Amidon and Associates, 1963; pp. 6-11, 26, and 27. Reprinted with permission of Edmund J. Amidon, Ned A. Flanders, and Paul S. Amidon and Associates.

Benjamin S. Bloom. "The Taxonomy of Educational Objectives and its Use in Curriculum Building." DEFINING EDUCATIONAL OBJECTIVES. C. M. Lindvall, editor. Pittsburgh: University of Pittsburgh Press, 1964. Reprinted with permission of the University of Pittsburgh Press.

Benjamin S. Bloom and others. TAXONOMY OF EDUCATIONAL OBJECTIVES, THE CLASSIFICATION OF EDUCATIONAL GOALS, HANDBOOK I: COGNITIVE DOMAIN. New York: David McKay, 1956. Reprinted with permission of David McKay, Inc.

Harry S. Broudy, B. O. Smith, and Joe R. Burnett. DEMOCRACY AND EXCELLENCE IN AMERICAN SECONDARY EDUCATION. Chicago: Rand McNally & Co., 1964; pp. 44, 46, 47, and 51. Reprinted with permission of Rand McNally & Co.

Ned A. Flanders. "Some Relationships Among Teacher Influence, Pupil Attitudes and Achievement." CONTEMPORARY RESEARCH ON TEACHER EFFECTIVENESS. Bruce J. Biddle and William J. Ellena, editors. New York: Holt, Rinehart, & Winston, 1964, pp. 142-148, 153-157. Reprinted with permission of Holt, Rinehart, & Winston.

N. L. Gage. "Paradigms for Research on Teaching." HANDBOOK OF RESEARCH ON TEACHING. Chicago: Rand McNally & Co., 1963; pp. 95-96. Reprinted with permission of the American Educational Research Association.

N. L. Gage. "Theories of Teaching." THEORIES OF LEARNING AND INSTRUCTION, 63rd YEARBOOK. Chicago: National Society for the Study of Education, 1964; p. 277. Reprinted with permission of the National Society for the Study of Education.

Albert E. Hickey and John M. Newton. THE LOGICAL BASIS OF TEACHING: I. THE EFFECT OF SUB-CONCEPT SEQUENCE ON LEARNING. Newburyport, Massachusetts: ENTELEK, 1964. Reprinted with permission of the Office of Naval Research and the authors.

David R. Krathwohl. "Stating Objectives Appropriately for Program, for Curriculum, and for Instructional Materials Development." *Journal of Teacher Education* 16, March 1965; pp. 84, 86-87. Reprinted with permission of *Journal of Teacher Education.*

David R. Krathwohl, Benjamin S. Bloom, and B. Masia. TAXONOMY OF EDUCATIONAL OBJECTIVES, THE CLASSIFICATION OF EDUCATIONAL GOALS, HANDBOOK II: AFFECTIVE DOMAIN. New York: David McKay, 1964. Reprinted with permission of David McKay, Inc.

Elizabeth Steiner Maccia. "Instructor as Influence Toward Rule-governed Behavior." THEORIES OF INSTRUCTION. James B. Macdonald and Robert R. Leeper, editors. Washington, D. C.: Association for Supervision and Curriculum Development, 1965, pp. 88, 89-90, 92-93, 98-99. Reprinted with permission of the Association for Supervision and Curriculum Development and Elizabeth Steiner Maccia. Copyright © 1965 by the Association for Supervision and Curriculum Development.

Hilda Taba. CURRICULUM DEVELOPMENT: THEORY AND PRACTICE. New York: Harcourt, Brace & World, 1962. Reprinted with permission of Hilda Taba.

Hilda Taba and James L. Hill. TEACHER HANDBOOK FOR CONTRA COSTA SOCIAL STUDIES, GRADES 1-6. Hayward, California: Rapid Printers and Lithographers, 1965; pp. 85, 113. Reprinted with permission of Hilda Taba.

Asahel D. Woodruff. "Characteristics of an Effective Instructional Unit." Working paper prepared for Academic Year Study, State University College, Geneseo, New York, April 14, 1966. Reprinted with permission of the author.

Asahel D. Woodruff. "Putting Subject Matter Into Conceptual Form." Paper delivered at TEAM project meeting, February 6, 1964. Reprinted with permission of the author.

Preface

This book is the result of an intensive academic year study into the theoretical foundations of teacher education of the future.[1] It was my pleasure to initiate and chair this study which brought thirteen of the nation's finest educational researchers and theoreticians together with the Division of Education of the State University College, Geneseo, New York. The Division of Education for the academic year study utilized as a guide to its investigation and thinking *A Proposal for the Revision of the Pre-Service Professional Component of a Program of Teacher Education* by Herbert F. LaGrone.[2] Dean LaGrone's *Proposal* represents a monumental and thoughtful effort at reviewing the available evidence and organizing it into a program for preparing teachers. Since the thinking was so good and the sources cited so outstanding, we chose various people from the *Proposal* as consultants to come to our campus about every two weeks throughout the academic year 1965-66 to present their ideas to us. As a result of a visit of two or three days by each of the specialists, we were better able to understand their work and the meaning it held for improved teacher education.

Before the consultants began coming to our campus, LaGrone spent two days with us discussing his *Proposal* and the nature of our study. From his guidance and discussion we embarked on our investigation. One point made quite clear to me by Dr. LaGrone was that we in Geneseo should attempt to "translate" our study into some form of workable document for other practicing teacher educators to use. Since our study was unique in nature, and since teacher education is under scrutiny now, I moved ahead in my attempt to formulate some document that could be used by other educators in the field. The thirteen consultants also offered their support and encouragement in the drafting of this document.

After considerable thinking and discussion with the thirteen consultants, the professional staff of The American Association of Colleges for Teacher Education, and others concerned with this writing project, it was decided that the document should take the form of a "resource book," whereby the work of our consultants would be stated in one volume for the consideration of others. Besides the research and theories of the consultants, there will be ideas presented on the implications of the work for improved teacher education. In this book, then, the objective presentation of the specialist's work and the meaning it has for new and different patterns of preparing teachers will be offered. From this presentation it is hoped that the reader will gather sufficient data and ideas to attempt to foster some kind of innovation in his teacher education program, or at least to do some serious thinking about preparing teachers. The work of the

[1] For a more complete discussion of the study see Verduin, John R., Jr. "Theoretical Foundations for Teacher Education of the Future: An Academic Year Study." *Journal of Teacher Education* 17: 112-14; Spring 1966.

[2] LaGrone, Herbert. *A Proposal for the Revision of the Pre-Service Professional Component of a Program of Teacher Education.* Washington, D. C.: The American Association of Colleges for Teacher Education, 1964.

thirteen consultants does not, of course, represent all of the significant work related to preparing teachers, but it does offer sufficient evidence for one to think about and perhaps to propose some change in existing programs.

I will make some introductory statements in Chapter One regarding teacher education and the nature of some of the variables associated with preparing good teachers. This should serve to start us thinking about preparatory programs and the meaning that each consultant's work has for them. The next thirteen chapters will present individually the work of the visiting consultants. The final chapter will offer some brief conclusions and directions as I view them. The conclusions will be only in regard to some commonality of ideas and summary of main points. Any conclusions regarding what teacher education should be as a result of this book will have to come from the reader. To be a true resource book, this must be the case. I will, however, suggest some directions that we in teacher education might take in our efforts to prepare better teachers for our public schools.

I should like to thank the State University of New York, Dr. Samuel B. Gould, president; and Dr. Harry Porter, provost, for granting me the funds for secretarial assistance and supplies to draft this resource book. I should also like to thank the State University College, Geneseo, New York; and Dr. Robert W. MacVittie, president, for providing funds for my salary during the writing project. Finally, I should like to thank The American Association of Colleges for Teacher Education for publishing this book. Only through the team efforts of these three major sources is this book possible.

This book also was made possible through the considerable efforts of our thirteen consultants. Very sincere appreciation must be expressed to them, not only for their assistance on this book, but for their contribution to the original study. Working with them during their visits to our campus was indeed challenging, enlightening, and most exciting. Their dedication to the educative process is of the highest, and their willingness to assist others contributes to their status as outstanding American educators.

Our consultants were as follows:

B. Othanel Smith, Professor of Education, University of Illinois
Hilda Taba, Professor of Education, San Francisco State College
N. L. Gage, Professor of Education and Psychology, Stanford University
Ned Flanders, Professor of Education, University of Michigan
Arno Bellack, Professor of Education, Teachers College, Columbia University
J. W. Getzels, Professor of Education and Psychology, University of Chicago
Harry Broudy, Professor of Education, University of Illinois
Albert Hickey, President, ENTELEK Incorporated, Newburyport, Massachusetts
James Gallagher, Professor of Education, University of Illinois
J. Richard Suchman, Research and Development Specialist, Science Research Associates
Asahel Woodruff, Professor of Education, University of Utah
David Krathwohl, Professor of Education and Dean, Syracuse University

Elizabeth Steiner Maccia, Professor and Chairman, Department of Philosophy, University of Southwestern Louisiana

I am also indebted to Miss Char Mae Akers for her considerable efforts at typing the various drafts of this manuscript and to my wife Janet for her assistance with editing and reviewing the tapes and manuscript.

Again, I must thank the staff of AACTE for the early guidance in this book, and Herbert LaGrone for his overall assistance in our study. The encouragement offered by these people and the professional staff of the Division of Education of the State University College, Geneseo, was most gratifying. It is our fervent hope that this book will contribute to the improvement of teacher education programs throughout the nation.

JRV, Jr.

Contents

Chapter 1. Introduction

The study of education and the careful rethinking about the preparation of teachers are perhaps at their highest point in history, and they should remain under critical study for some time. The writing of James B. Conant[1] has prompted professional teacher educators to think critically about programs that prepare young people for a career in teaching. If one accepts the notions of Conant, however, he might automatically conclude that there is no body of knowledge, no content, and no discipline in education or that none can be developed. To concede this would be pure folly on the part of professional educators. There is enough data on the topic now to start formulating some different kinds of patterns for preparing a more analytical and critical person to assume the position of classroom teacher.

If one were to analyze teacher education now, it would not be difficult to find that the typical undergraduate program for teachers consists of foundations courses, methods courses, and a form of practicum. Does this produce the kind of critical, decision-making person necessary for teaching in our schools now and in the future? It may not be too difficult to answer no to this proposition.

What is known about the teaching act, knowledge and order of content, educational objectives, thinking and concept formation, and theories and paradigms for teaching? Further, what is known about the analysis of these important functions in our preparatory programs? Are we giving them proper consideration, or are we relying on the "intuitive" person to carry on the functions of classroom teaching in our public schools? Reliance on the intuitive person suggests that there is no distinct area of teacher education and that there never will be. This, too, is wrong, and many teacher education people are beginning to realize it.

To change these false notions, perhaps it will take the efforts more of practicing teacher educators than of the educational researchers and

---

[1] Conant, James B. *The Education of American Teachers.* New York: McGraw-Hill Book Co., 1963.

theoreticians to foster the needed change in preparatory programs. The change must occur in the college classrooms throughout the nation, for change at this grass roots level is what is needed for new designs in teacher education.

The early research by Smith (see Chapter 2) has opened the door to study of the teaching act. Others have taken up the task so that now we have some data on teaching strategies and the analysis of classroom interaction. Still others have provided some paradigms, guides, and theories of teaching and formal classroom instruction. One can glean from the literature some significant ideas on teaching, the analysis of teaching, and theoretical notions about teaching. These outstanding studies should assist the teacher educator in his search for better ways of preparing teachers.

One is confronted with the use, order, and structure of the vast explosion of knowledge and what meaning it now has for the young people in our public schools. Teachers must consider how content can be ordered and used properly for effective meaning in the classroom to insure that learning takes place to a higher degree. Teacher educators should first give consideration to the studies and thinking in this all-important area.

In this age of rapid social change and perplexing world problems, one is quite interested in the development of thinking on the part of the youngsters in our schools. How is one taught to think and inquire? What are the important goals in the cognitive domain? How can one achieve these goals as well as those of the affective domain? How can adequate concept formation be fostered in our youngsters, and what is necessary for this kind of concept formation? These seem to be important concerns facing young people who will become teachers, as well as those who teach teachers. There is substantial data and thinking on these important areas, and after a careful consideration, it should find its way into the preparatory programs of teachers.

To develop a program for the preparation of teachers requires a considerable effort on the part of the teacher educators. It requires a decision on what is important for teachers, an identification of the variables for consideration, and some theoretical and perhaps some philosophical notions about teaching-learning and the meaning it has for teachers.

There are three major areas to consider when thinking about the preparation of teachers: general education, specialized education, and the professional component. Although the first area may be beyond the realm of this book, teacher educators must consider what goes into this area for the preparation of better teachers. Since the school in which the teacher will teach is found in a cultural setting, then perhaps some sociology and history are necessary. Since the outcomes from the educative process are philosophical, some philosophy may be important. Since we live in a highly technical society, perhaps some study of the sciences is imperative. These arguments could be built for humanities, arts, and other disciplines within the area of general education and, of course, require decisions on the part of the interested teacher educator. What seems important for future teachers for effective teaching and effective living within a democratic society?

Some decisions must also be made concerning specialized teachers. Should the history teacher be required to take enough work in history to think like an historian? Should this depth be required of teachers who work in other major discipline areas? What should be required of the elementary school teacher in specialized areas? How much depth in content should he have to perform his duty as an effective teacher? Again, what study in social sciences, science, humanities, arts, and special areas in education is necessary for the effective function of a classroom teacher? Since this area is more closely related to the professional education component, teacher educators must give serious thought to it. Parts of the remaining chapters of this book will allude to this important area.

Finally, the professional component, or selected experiences developed for the prospective teacher to prepare him for his professional work in the classroom, is of vital concern to the teacher educator.

Before a program of professional experiences can be identified and tested with teacher education students, some philosophical questions have to be answered; and some assumptions about the students, the program or content, and the outcomes should be made. First of all, when thinking about a preparatory program, one must begin by thinking about the kind of product he desires. What results does he want from his intensive work with future teachers? What skills, abilities, and knowledge should the future teacher possess after completing the program?

What assumptions can be made regarding the student's background, ability to learn, current conceptual scheme, and changes in behavior? What does the teacher educator think about knowledge, learning, and new media in relation to a program for teachers? A careful examination of these and other factors must be made when thinking about preparing teachers.

To serve as a guide to the thinking about the preparation of teachers, the Geneseo Study utilized the *Proposal* by Herbert LaGrone.[2] This *Proposal* made a significant attempt to structure a program for teachers based on existing literature in education. LaGrone suggested his assumptions, made some philosophical judgments, and then proceeded to plot the program. The *Proposal* was indeed only a proposal to create study, thinking, and interest on the problem of preparing teachers. *Conceptual Models in Teacher Education* is a study of parts of the *Proposal,* and LaGrone's work served as a guide to the writing of the present volume. To enhance the reader's knowledge about the subject, perhaps he may wish to read the *Proposal* during the coverage of this book. Too, the *Proposal* may offer to the reader some basic notions of what is involved in a new and different proposal for preparing teachers.

Within Course I, The Analytical Study of Teaching, of LaGrone's

[2] LaGrone, Herbert F. *A Proposal for the Revision of the Pre-Service Professional Component of a Program of Teacher Education.* Washington, D. C.: The American Association of Colleges for Teacher Education, 1964.

Proposal, this resource book will include the work by B. Othanel Smith on the Logical Aspects of Teaching. This will be followed by Hilda Taba's work on Teaching Strategies for Cognitive Growth, which resulted from her investigation of Thinking in Elementary School Children. Then a discussion on Paradigms and Theories for Teaching by N. L. Gage from his extensive writing in this area will be offered. The analysis of classroom interaction of the teacher and students will be discussed using Ned Flanders' Interaction Analysis research. Then the extensive, descriptive study, The Language of the Classroom, by Arno Bellack will be reviewed. Finally, within Course I, the Classroom Group and the School as a Social System by J. W. Getzels will be offered. From a study of these six outstanding efforts the reader can perhaps devise some means for analysis of the many variables associated with teaching, and then move to the concept formation stage. Using these various works should permit the student to identify, explain, and even demonstrate the important concepts. Sufficient concrete examples in these works should also provide the necessary means for analysis and concept formation.

Within Course II, Structures and Uses of Knowledge, the Uses of Knowledge by Harry S. Broudy will be discussed in this book. Following Broudy's work will be the work of Albert E. Hickey on the Logical Structure of Teaching. From these two works the teacher educator, and in turn the teacher education student, can begin to look at the logical organization of the content to be taught. Also, they may be better able to analyze the content and place it in better order for teaching. From the work of these specialists one can begin to make better decisions about what should be taught and the particular order of the teaching.

Under Course III, Concepts of Human Development and Learning, comes a discussion of the works by James Gallagher, J. Richard Suchman, and Asahel Woodruff. Gallagher used the Structure of the Intellect in some of his research on Gifted Children and thus has seen the meaning of this three-dimensional cognitive model. Suchman's work has been focused on the process of Inquiry Training and what meaning this has for the individual and his conceptual system. Woodruff's very significant work on Concept Formation and the prerequisites for adequate formation of concepts will be presented and discussed to show its meaning for the teaching process. A careful examination of the works of these three specialists should assist the teacher education professor and student in thinking about intellectual development, inquiry, and concept formation.

Course IV, Designs for Teaching-Learning, in the *Proposal* is discussed within the frameworks of the works of Woodruff and Krathwohl. Woodruff's additional work on Learning Unit Design will be covered in this book, and a discussion on Education Goals by David Krathwohl will be offered. These two efforts will assist the teacher educator in preparing for a method of teaching utilizing many of the other specialists' works. The teacher education student should be able to prepare a learning experience for the adequate development of concepts.

Under Course V, Demonstration and Evaluation of Teaching Competencies, this book will present the work of Elizabeth Steiner Maccia on Theories of Formal Instruction. A discussion of this work will aid the teacher in thinking about theoretical models and in developing a theory of formal instruction.

It should be noted that several of the studies of the consultants can apply to other areas or courses as outlined by LaGrone. This is why the reader should perhaps consider both LaGrone's *Proposal* and this book concurrently.

The writer does not suggest a close adherence to the notions of the *Proposal*. Only after a complete study of the topics in this book and some additional thinking and review should the reader suggest and test a method of preparing teachers which will offer the outcomes desired by him. It is to this point that this book is written. Completely new programs as well as modification within existing programs can be cited as the goals of this book. Closure and conclusions must, therefore, come from the reader.

Chapter 2. The Logical Aspects of Teaching

Professor B. Othanel Smith[1] and associates conducted some extensive inquiry into the logical dimensions of teaching under a United States Office of Education grant. The context of this research will be reported here, and the implications of this work for improved teacher education programs will be discussed.

This research was an outgrowth of some earlier investigatory work into the proposition of whether or not instruction in logic in selected high school subjects would change the ability of students to think critically. The goals of this research project were defined broadly as:

1. Devising a procedure for finding out whether or not there are logical dimensions of teaching and for describing such dimensions as discovered.
2. Determining if there is any significant difference in the behavior of those trained in the logical dimensions of teaching from those not trained.
3. Determining the effects of such different behavior as may be found upon the logical behavior of the students.

Only the description of the logical dimensions of teaching behavior will be discussed in this chapter. The research reported in this chapter is the first level of inquiry, where behaviors are observed, described, and classified; and thus no change in the behavior is prescribed. From a variety of alternatives Smith chose two elements of the conceptual context to study: verbal behavior and the logical nature of the behavior. He wanted to analyze student-teacher-content interaction in logical terms. Teaching behavior as described by Smith is multifaceted, but he selected only the behavior that induces learning as an end product. Since teaching behavior is primarily verbal in nature, he studied only verbal behavior, such as spoken and written discourse and symbolic expression. He selected logic

[1] Dr. Smith is Professor of Education at the University of Illinois in the Bureau of Educational Research.

because questions entail logical operations. A logical operation is a verbal performance, the correctness of which can be ascertained by the degree to which it corresponds to the requirements of logic.

Smith suggests that there are three types of verbal behavior used in teaching. One type, such as instructing, eliciting responses, and causing the topic to be remembered, is intended to have a specific effect. This kind of discourse involves such intellectual operations as explaining and defining so that the topic can be understood and restated. The second kind of verbal behavior, simply telling the student how to perform an operation, can be checked if the student is able to perform the skill or operation required of him. Once the skill is acquired, then nothing more is required. The third kind of verbal behavior, such as praising, advising, and commending the student, has an emotional rather than a cognitive influence on the student. These kinds of utterances are not usually of an intellectual nature, but are used for affective purposes.

Smith further defines two kinds of behaviors that may be considered logical in a sense. Behavior is logical if it can be formulated symbolically in a logical form, and it can be logical if it can be modified in response to a self-analysis and correction of one's thought processes in accordance with the rules of logic. These two notions about logical behavior are used in this research.

Smith and associates gathered their data through the taping of secondary classroom discourse. Their unit of discourse was divided simply into two forms: episode and monologue.

Episode was the unit used when more than one speaker addressed the group. Generally the episodic discourse would go through a three-phase pattern: the opening (generally a question), the sustaining (generally a reply or judgment), and the closing (an affirmative remark). Some episodes did not go through the final stage because of a lack of a closing comment; they could move back to the opening or sustaining phase.

Monologue discourse was used extensively for making assignments and announcements and for giving directions. It occurred much less frequently than did episodic discourse.

For the development of categories into which the various episodes could be placed, Smith found that the conventional categories of logic would not work completely because of the great variety and complexity of symbolic operations demanded by teachers. Therefore, some unusual categories of logic were used, and of course, the influence of the conventional categories found its way into the final category system. Certain considerations finally led to classifying episodes by their opening phases.

The opening phase always contained a verbal move that evoked at least one and many times a series of related verbal exchanges. The verbal move was termed an "entry" by Smith. The entry was a self-initiating move on the part of the person who made it, and it was followed by some responding remarks. The entry, it was argued, thus tended to shape the nature of the episode. From the classification of the entry one could then determine the logic of the response or sustaining phase.

The categories into which the entries were grouped are:

DEFINING. Entries making up this group are concerned with how words or other symbols are used to refer to objects (abstract or concrete). These entries vary in form and content, but, in general, they ask implicitly or explicitly for the meaning of terms.

Defining may take the following forms: (a) A term is given and a definition or meaning of the term is to be supplied as a response to the entry; for example, "What does the word 'dorsal' mean?" (b) The entry contains neither the word "mean" nor the word "define." The entry asks instead what something *is*—for example, "What is a cablegram?" (c) The noun in the entry is a grammatically proper name. In these cases, the entry requires that the object designated by the proper name be described or otherwise indicated—for example, "Who was Paul Elmer More?" (d) Some entries ask for a term or expression that can be substituted for another term or expression—for example, "What is the symbol for gravity?"

DESCRIBING. To describe is to represent something by words or drawing, to tell about something. Thus, the entries making up this category mention or suggest something and require that an account of this something be given. In the question, "What can you tell us about the gill rakers?" it is clear that we are asked to describe the gill rakers.

However, not all questions that mention or allude to something ask for a description. "What would be some examples of a sense organ?" is a question that names a class of things and asks that examples be cited. No description is requested.

In some cases, as in the example just given, it is easy to tell whether or not the entry requires a description or an identification; but in a large number of entries, this intent is obscure. "What did Cleveland find out?" is a question that might be answered by naming whatever it was that Cleveland uncovered, but the expectations would be more nearly satisfied were the question answered by a brief *account* of what he found out. On the other hand, "What is a common defect of this part (cerebellum) of the brain?" may be answered by naming the defect, although a description of the defect would not be inappropriate as an answer.

DESIGNATING. To designate is to identify something by name—word or other symbol. The name designates the object (abstract or concrete) to which it refers. Thus, this group of entries is made up of items in which something is described or otherwise indicated, and the name used to refer to it or to identify it is requested. These entries vary widely in form and content. In general, they demand that objects (abstract or concrete) be designated by name or other symbol or simply by pointing. Consider the question, "What do you call a word used to modify a verb?" The question is answered by giving the name of the word—namely, "adverb." The question, "What reptile did he show in the film?" is answered in the same way—by giving a name—although the question does not explicitly ask what the reptile is called. Again, "What is the word (in a given sentence) that is to be modified?" is a question that can be answered by pointing to the particular word or by saying it.

Designating may take the following forms: (a) The entry demands that an example or instance, or a number of examples of a group of things be named; (b) The entry gives a set of things and requires that all members of the set be named; (c) The entry gives a particular class or group of things, or a particular object, and requires that it be specified by name or by pointing; (d) The entry describes or suggests something and asks explicitly for its name.

STATING. Entries in this group do not ask for names, descriptions, and so forth, but for things to be stated. They may ask for statements of issues, steps in proofs, rules, obligations, theorems, conclusions, ideas, beliefs, promises, threats. For example, the question, "What is the conclusion?" asks for a statement of some sort. It seldom can be answered satisfactorily merely naming or describing.

REPORTING. The entries in this group ask for a report on what a book or document says, for information in the text, or for a summary or review, for example, "What happens in Chapter Ten?"

SUBSTITUTING. The entries making up this category ask the student to perform a symbolic operation, usually of a mathematical nature, for example, "Substitute y for x in this equation."

EVALUATING. To evaluate is to estimate the worth, dependability, or the like, of something. An entry of this type requires that some object, expression, event, action, or state of affairs be rated on its value, dependability, desirability, and the like. For example, the question, "Is he a good judge?" asks the student to rate a judge who acts in some particular manner.

OPINING. To opine is to express beliefs, usually based on little or no evidence. Such beliefs are about what is possible, what might have been and is not, what might obtain in the future. "Do you think that historians will say that Wilson was right in proposing the League of Nations?" is an entry that asks for conjecture about how historians of the future will judge Woodrow Wilson with respect to a particular set of actions—those involved in proposing the League of Nations.

CLASSIFYING. Each entry in this group makes explicit reference to an instance and/or class (group, set, kind) of things. The entry requires that a given instance be put in a larger class to which it belongs as a subclass. For example, "What special type of triangle did you find it to be?" is a question that makes reference, by the word "it," to a particular triangle. The student is expected to tell to what class of triangles this particular one belongs. As an illustration of questions that ask for a class to be placed in a larger class, consider the following: "What group of animals does the jellyfish belong to?" In this question, the term "jellyfish" does not refer to a particular jellyfish, but to a subclass. The student is required to name the larger class to which the group of animals called "jellyfish" belongs.

COMPARING AND CONTRASTING. This type of entry requires comparison of two or more things (actions, factors, objects, processes, and so on). There are three kinds of entries in this category: (a) The entry merely asks for a comparison, the points of comparison not being explicitly indicated, for example, "What is the difference between probation and parole?" (b) The entry specifies two (or more) things and asks that either their similarities or differences be noted with respect to a particular characteristic, for example, "Is its (fish's) eye very large compared to the size of the grasshopper's?" (c) The entry names a thing and requires that another thing similar to it, or different from it, be indicated; for instance, "Which one (Canadian house) corresponds to the House of Commons?"

CONDITIONAL INFERRING. This category consists of entries each containing an antecedent—that is, the conditional parts of a statement. In the sentence, "When it rains, the streets are wet," the phrase "when it rains" is the antecedent. The phrase "the streets are wet" is the consequent. Now, the entries that make up this category give an antecedent. Sometimes they give both an antecedent and a consequent. They never contain a consequent alone.

Here is an example of an entry containing an antecedent only: "How does that (undemocratic handling of colonies) affect the mother country?" The phrase "undemocratic handling of colonies" is the antecedent. It describes the condition of which the effect on the mother country is the consequent. The question asks the student to tell what the consequent is. Take another case: "If the diagonal (in a rhombus) is given as 12 and this angle is 60, what is the angle at C and at A?" In all cases where the antecedent alone is given, the entry requires that the consequent—effect, result, outcome, subsequent behavior—be supplied as the answer.

Consider an example of an entry containing both an antecedent and a consequent: "Did you ever get a headache from sleeping in a draft?" The phrase "sleeping in a draft" is the antecedent and "get a headache" is the consequent. In entries of this kind, the student is required to affirm the consequent, to deny it, or to say he does not know if he has ever suffered or enjoyed the consequent under the given condition.

Some of these entries ask for value judgments; some ask for statements of result or outcome; and others for descriptions of actions, decisions, and the like.

EXPLAINING. There are several types of explanation entries, all of which have one thing in common: They give a particular consequent and they require that an antecedent be supplied. To explain is to set forth an antecedent condition of which the particular event to be explained is taken as the effect—or else, to give the rules, definitions, or facts used to justify decisions, judgments, actions, and so on. In the example, "Why did the light go out?" the consequent is "the light go out." The question asks the student to give a reason or reasons to account for the fact that the light is out. The reasons(s) is (are) the antecedent(s).

There are six kinds of explanation entries, depending upon the kind of antecedent—mechanical, causal, sequent, procedural, teleological, and normative—used to account for the consequent. These are described as follows:

Mechanical-explaining entries give an event or action that must be accounted for through description of the way the parts of a structure fit or work together. For example, "How do fish make a sound?" asks for a description of the mechanism or structure that enables the fish to make vibrations.

Entries of the causal-explaining type give events, situations, or states to be accounted for and ask that a state of affairs be cited of which the given event (or a situation or state) is taken to be the result. For instance, "What makes a person's muscles 'twitch'?" asks for a description of the condition of the nerves associated with twitching.

Sequent-explaining entries ask how something happened. They require that a sequence of events be cited of which the event to be accounted for is the end point. For example, as already cited, the question, "How did McKinley happen to be killed," requires the recitation of events leading up to the assassination of President McKinley.

Procedural-explaining entries require description of the steps or operations by which a given result or end is attained. Here is a sample of entry: "How did you get 72 (for an answer)?" The student is expected to tell the steps he took to obtain his answer.

The teleological-explaining type of entry contains descriptions of actions, decisions, states of affairs, or the worth of things, and requires that these be accounted for or justified by reference to purposes, functions, or goals. For instance, "Why are you doing those problems?" asks for a purpose—such as satisfying an assignment.

Entries of the normative-explaining type do either of two things. First, they may mention or assume a decision, judgment, or state of knowing and require that it be justified by citation of a definition or characteristic or both. For example, "Why do we call them (animals between vertebrates and invertebrates) the *chordata* animal group?" asks that the student give a definition of the *chordata* phylum and point out that the animals in question have the characteristics called for by the definition. Second, members of this group of entries cite actions, decisions, or choices (either made or to be made) and require that rules be given as reasons for the decisions, choices, etc. For example, "Why do we use 'shorter' (in comparing two pencils as to length)?" asks for a rule prescribing the use of "shorter" in such cases. Entries of this type usually call for grammatical or mathematical rules.

DIRECTING AND MANAGING CLASSROOM. Many questions asked by teachers have little or no logical significance. They are not designed to evoke thought but to keep the classroom activities moving along.[2]

Observations[3] from this investigation tended to indicate that the performance by teachers and students is of low quality when judged by logical standards. The handling of the content of instruction by both students and teachers is at a common sense level. There is no more clarity and rigor of thought and analysis in classroom discourse than is ordinarily found in the casual give and take of discussion occurring anywhere in daily life. Further, teachers do not understand the logic of discussion or the logic of subject matter. Smith also found that the treatment of concepts, principles, and other knowledge often lacked clarity and rigor. Some examples by Smith can be cited to display the fact that teaching behavior seldom conforms to strict logical structures or the ideal forms found in logic.

Teaching behavior seldom exhibits complete logical explanations. Instead of complete explanations, we find episodes consisting of explanation sketches that either fail to give the connecting facts or, as is more often the case, the explanatory principle. The following are typical cases of elliptical explanations in the classroom.

1. A passage from a chemistry text is read defining acids, bases, and salts. Examples of these are given, along with some of their commercial uses. It is pointed out that lead is used as a base in many paints and that lead is most often found, in nature, combined with sulphur as lead sulphate. After some further elaboration the teacher asks, "Why does lead-base paint turn black?" A student replies that the lead combines (with sulphur). The pattern of explanation may be diagrammed in this way:

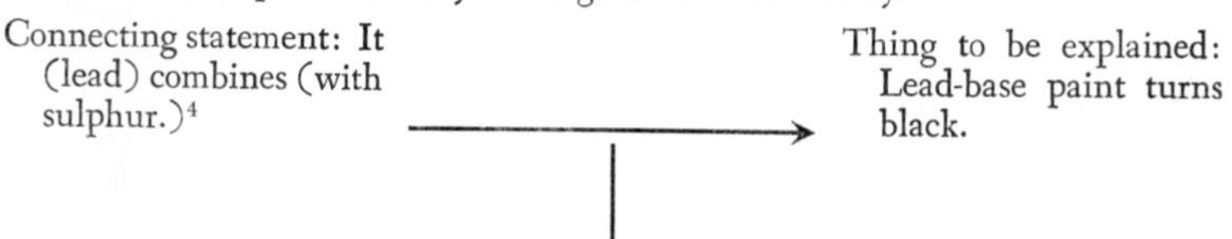

Explanatory principle: (If lead in paint combines with sulphur in the air, it forms a black substance called lead sulphate.)

2. A class in history is discussing Cleveland's second administration. They are considering several unpopular things (at least, unpopular with certain groups of people) that Cleveland did during his second term in office. The teacher asks, "What did he (Cleveland) do that made the capitalists

[2] Meux and Smith (1), pp. 142-148.

[3] For reliability, experimental procedures, data, and other pertinent information on this research see Smith and Meux (2).

[4] Parentheses indicate what teacher and student assumed but did not say.

unhappy?" A student says that he repealed the tariffs. The pattern is as follows:

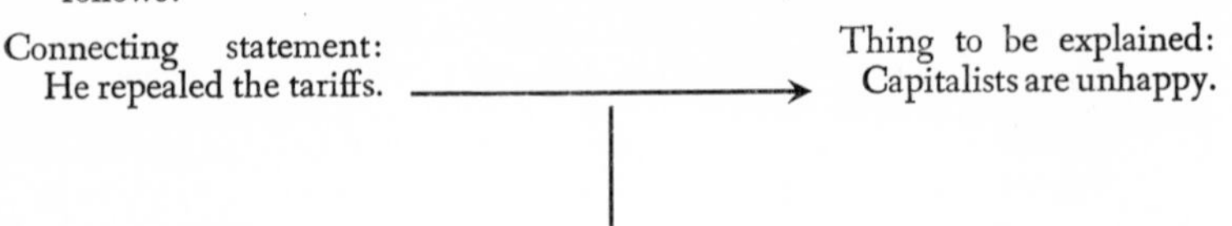

Explanatory principle: (If tariffs are repealed, capitalists are dissatisfied and unhappy.)

In each of these cases the explanatory principle is missing. Absence of an explanation sketch is not to be understood as indicating a poor explanation. There are, doubtless, many cases in which the principle is so clearly understood that to repeat it would be redundant. In still other cases, the principle is trivial and does not bear repeating. In some cases, however, the principle is at the heart of the explanatory process, and failure to make it clear is to give a faulty explanation. In dealing with the problem of finding the area of a rhombus where one angle is 60° and the shorter diagonal is twelve units long, the question arises as to how the class knows that an indicated angle is 120°. The student says that opposite angles in a rhombus are equal. If the principles were not given in this case, the explanation would be faulty because the correct principle is neither obvious nor understood from the context. Diagrammatically the pattern is as follows:

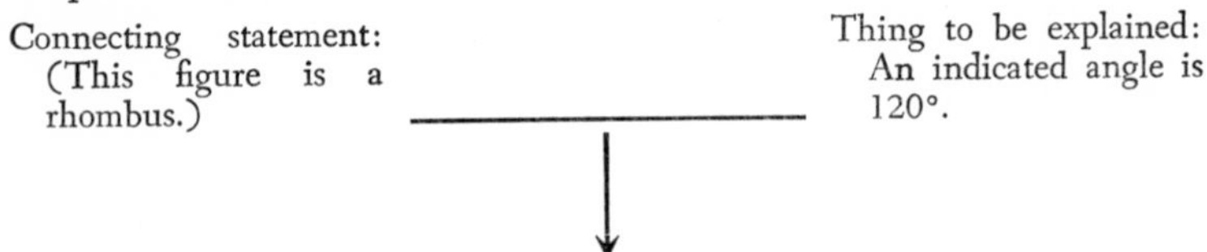

Explanatory principle: Opposite angles in a rhombus are equal.

In its ideal form, valuation dimension consists of four factors: (a) something—object, statement or expression, event, action, state of affairs—to be rated as good or bad, just or unjust, true or false, acceptable or unacceptable, and so on; (b) a rating; (c) a criterion or set of criteria by which the rating is made; and (d) facts about the thing to be rated that support the use of the criterion in making the rating. Suppose a class is discussing the question of whether or not certain statements that appear in so-called "true stories" are indeed true. To answer this question logically, the students must have a criterion for truth. In this case, the criterion they decide to use is that any statement conforming to observations is true. The set of statements appearing in the stories are to be rated as true or false. To apply the criterion to the statements is to get evidence that the statements are true—that is, that the statements correspond to observations. If there is such evidence, then the statements may be rated as true.

Valuation episodes, almost without exception, are elliptical. Either the criterion is not given, or the facts are missing. The following episode illustrates a valuative structure in which the criterion is not given. The class has been discussing the differential treatment accorded the Philippines, Cuba, and Puerto Rico after the Spanish-American War. The teacher asks, "Were Cubans really better prepared to take on the responsibilities of governing themselves than the other two groups?" A student answers that the Cubans were more prepared and adds that the Puerto Rican people did not have very much experience in self-government. In diagrammatic form, the structure of the episode looks like this:

Rating: Cubans were more (better) prepared.

Thing to be rated: Preparation of Cubans for self-government in comparison to Philippinos and Puerto Ricans.

Facts: The Puerto Rican people did not have much experience in self-government. (Supposedly the Cubans did, and nothing is said about the Philippinos.)

Criterion: Not given.

In the foregoing case, the criterion is entirely missing, and the facts on which to rest a value judgment are only partially cited. This example is typical of valuative episodes as they actually occur in teaching situations, although other elliptical forms often occur. In one of these, a rating is given without the justifying facts and criterion. In discussing a novel, the class is comparing one of the characters–Scobie–with Christ. The teacher suggests that Christ's weakness, from a human standpoint, was his goodness. Then she asks, "What is Scobie's main weakness?" A student answers, "It is sympathy (with mankind)." The teacher says, "All right." The logical structure of the episode is:

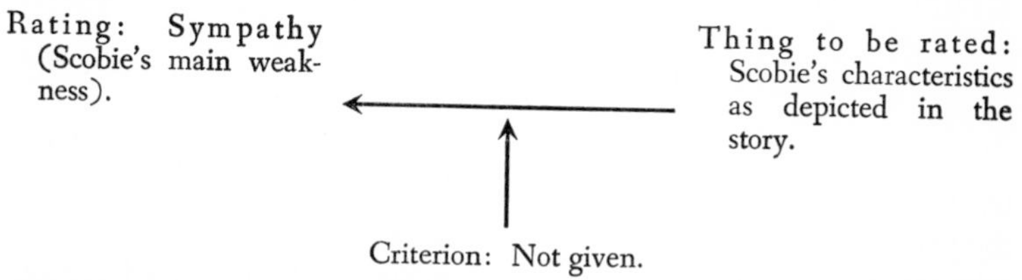

Here, it is clear that neither fact nor criterion is given. There is no justification whatever of the rating–but only agreement between the teacher's judgment and the student's.

An infrequent incomplete form occurs when the evaluation criterion is given without any facts connecting the criterion with the rating. In discussing a novel, the teacher asks, "Is it fair for an author to use emotional appeal to promote an argument?" A student says that it is fair and then goes on to announce the criterion on which he wishes to rest his rating. The skeletonized form of the episode is as follows:

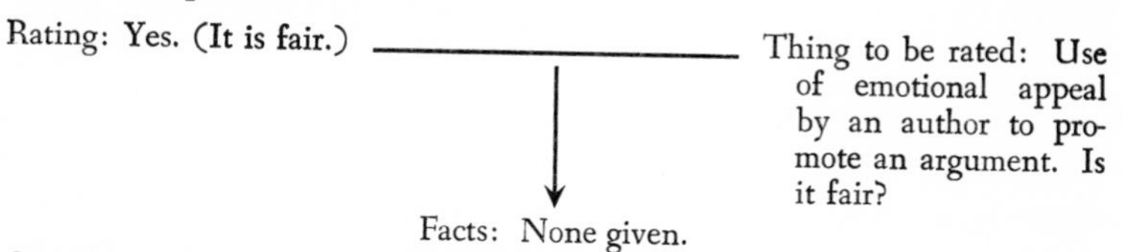

Criterion: Student A. If things appeal emotionally, then you can get people interested.

Student B. Once you get people interested, then you can appeal to their reason.[5]

---

[5] Meux and Smith (1), pp. 153-157.

Implications for Improved Teacher Education

From the above brief discussion of the intensive work of Smith, one can glean several important implications for preparing teachers. It should be noted here that Smith has moved beyond his study to a study of the strategies of teaching, utilizing the original work.[6] From the second study he hopes to develop the "if . . . , then" proposition for selected strategies for teaching concepts and other elements such as reasons, procedures, and values. Since the second study has not been completed at this writing, it is not mentioned here. At the time of the completion of the second study, one will be able to better understand the implications of this work in the logical dimensions of teaching for improved teacher education. However, several important concerns are present now.

First of all, as suggested by LaGrone in his *Proposal,* Smith's work could be used as an analytical instrument to assess the teaching behavior of preservice students. The preservice teacher could teach a single concept to a limited number of students. His instruction could then be followed by an analysis of a tape to determine the degree of his success in teaching a concept. After the analysis, some reteaching could occur with appropriate corrective measures. This would afford the analytical determinant to teaching behavior which is the theme of LaGrone's *Proposal* and parts of this book. The analysis aspect of this work could occur in the usual methods courses or perhaps could find its way into a theory and laboratory course on teaching.

Since Smith's study indicates poor logical operation on the part of teachers in handling content, this research takes on additional meaning for the usual methods courses. Courses in methods should examine the twelve different types of logical processes or operations developed by Smith and indicate the most effective ways of performing them. This activity has to be done in relation to the particular subject matter being taught, because the handling of the various operations may vary from one discipline to another. For example, explanation in one discipline would be different from that in another. Although there are common logical elements in the different ways of explaining, there is sufficient difference in the performance of the explanatory operation in various content areas to warrant individual treatment in each area. This specialization must apply to all logical processes performed by teachers and pupils in the classroom. Smith suggests that the study of the twelve logical operations of teaching as seen by him is more appropriate than a formal course in logic. The latter approach might be wasteful, since about two-thirds of a course in logic may not be applicable to teaching. Since the hypothesis of this extensive research was that the quality of instruction would improve if the logical operations involved improved, an extensive study of the basic operations seems desirable by the preservice teacher education student.

Perhaps the major significant implication for utilizing Smith's work

---

[6] See Smith, and others (4).

in teacher education programs evolves when attention is given to the possible outcomes for students in the classroom of the teacher working with logical operations. Smith feels it is reasonable to suppose that students of teachers whose behavior measures high in logical operations would show higher scores on critical thinking tests than those of teachers having lower ratings, assuming, of course, that all other conditions are equal. Another expectation suggested by Smith is that students of teachers who are superior in the handling of logical operations would rate high in the ability to identify mistakes in reasoning, in defining, in valuating, and in other logical processes. Further, the improvement in the teacher's ability to handle these operations would result in more student knowledge. Besides learning the usual facts, the student would learn the new relationships that proper performance of logical operations brings out. Finally, he would learn the laws of a discipline, how laws are used in giving explanations of phenomena, and how they are tied together in a system of definitions and theories. It would be difficult to argue with the values of these goals for forthright instruction in a classroom.

Therefore, if we want increased knowledge and the ability to think critically as outcomes of instruction, and if teachers can achieve these outcomes by improving their abilities to handle logical operations, then it would be logical for teacher educators to examine and incorporate some of Smith's work in their teacher preparation program.

Bibliography

1. Meux, Milton O. and Smith, B. Othanel. "Logical Dimensions in Teaching Behavior." *Contemporary Research on Teacher Effectiveness.* Edited by Bruce J. Biddle and William J. Ellena. New York: Holt, Rinehart & Winston. Chapter 5, pp. 127-164.

2. Smith, B. Othanel and Meux, Milton O. *A Study of the Logic of Teaching.* (Cooperative Project No. 258, U. S. Department of Health, Education, and Welfare, Office of Education.) Urbana, Illinois: University of Illinois, 1962.

3. ———, and Ennis, Robert H. *Language and Concepts in Education.* Chicago: Rand McNally & Co., 1961.

4. ———, and others. *A Tentative Report on the Strategies of Teaching.* (Cooperative Project No. 1640, U. S. Department of Health, Education, and Welfare, Office of Education.) Urbana, Illinois: University of Illinois, 1964.

5. ———. "The Need for Logic in Methods Courses." *Theory Into Practice* 3: 5-8; February 1964.

Chapter 3. Teaching Strategies for Cognitive Growth

Professor Hilda Taba[1] and associates have focused their intensive research largely on the development of a strategy for the generation and enhancement of independent thought processes on the part of elementary school children in the area of social studies. The central goal for the study was to examine the development of thought under three training conditions: (a) a curriculum designed for the development of thought, (b) teaching strategies focused explicitly and consciously on the mastery of the necessary cognitive skills, and (c) a sufficient time span to permit a developmental sequence in training.[2] A subsidiary objective was to develop a method of categorizing thought processes for analyzing thinking as it occurs in a classroom setting. A further subsidiary goal was to develop the teaching strategies for the development of cognitive skills. However, the transaction between teaching acts and student behavior was a significant aspect of the analysis of this work.

The essence of this chapter on Taba's work will focus on the thought processes or cognitive tasks as defined by her and the teaching strategies needed for the mastery of these cognitive skills. To ignore the curriculum aspect of this research is ill advised, but it is felt that once understood and mastered, the thought processes and strategies can be utilized in any type of the curriculum and even in areas other than the social studies area (the focus of this research). Therefore, the processes involved will be discussed with an understanding that the curriculum content is an essential ingredient for the successful execution of the processes. The social studies curriculum will be brought out only to afford meaning to the important cognitive processes.[3]

---

[1] Dr. Taba is Professor of Education at San Francisco State College.

[2] Taba, Levine, and Elzey (3).

[3] For reliability, experimental procedures, data, and other pertinent information, see Taba, Levine, and Elzey (3).

Taba identified three categories of thought processes or cognitive tasks: (a) concept formation, (b) interpretation of data and the making of inferences, and (c) the application of known principles and facts to explain new phenomena, to predict consequences from known conditions and events, or to develop hypotheses by using known generalizations and facts.[4] These three cognitive tasks were analyzed from two different angles: the operations or elements involved, and the sequential steps necessary for mastering them.

Concept Formation

Since concept formation is considered the basic form of cognition on which all cognitive processes depend, Taba, for her study, utilized basic concept formation and defined it as consisting of three different processes or operations: (a) the differentiation of the specific properties of objects or events, such as differentiating the materials of which houses are built from other characteristics of houses (this differentiation involves the process of analysis, in the sense of breaking down the global complexes representing objects and events into specified properties); (b) grouping, or a process of assembling specified properties across many objects and events, i.e., grouping together hospitals, doctors, and medicine according to some semi-intuitively identifiable basis such as representing something to do with health, or the fact that their availability serves as an index for the standard of living; and (c) labeling or categorizing; i.e., explicitly identifying the basis for grouping, and subsuming the items under some label or category.[5]

In the classroom differentiation may be called for in the act of enumeration, either by recall from previous experience, or by specifying items noted in a complex presentation, such as a film or a story. For example, students could list the materials used for building houses, or name things and events noted in a film. Grouping is putting together diverse items which have some common characteristics, such as grouping schools, hospitals, and parks as community facilities. Usually, this process of searching for a basis of grouping leads to a discovery that the items can be grouped in multiple ways, depending on the purpose and the basis used.

Categorization occurs in the form of making decisions about what labels to use for groups, what to subsume under which category, such as whether weather is to be subsumed under climate, or vice versa. This involves an awareness of orders of subordination and superordination.

In teaching these operations, as well as in analyzing them, the hierarchical nature of concepts must be kept in mind. As the process of abstracting continues, the categories or labels become increasingly more abstract and encompassing, and thereby more remote from the initial concrete reference. This increasing abstraction also enhances their power as cognitive tools for organizing information. In the classroom, concepts on different levels of abstraction may be suggested simultaneously, which

---

[4] Taba (6).

[5] *Ibid.*

creates the problem of differentiation. For example, students may enumerate materials for building housing in specific terms, such as tar paper and fiber glass, or in classes, such as insulation.

A graphic representation of the cognitive task of concept formation and the skills for using it appears below:

Concept Formation[6]

Overt Activity	*Covert Mental Operation*	*Eliciting Questions*
1. Enumeration and listing	1. Differentiation	1. What did you see? hear? note?
2. Grouping	2. Identifying common properties, abstracting	2. What belongs together? On what criterion?
3. Labeling, categorizing	3. Determining the hierarchical order of items. Super- and sub-ordination.	3. How would you call these groups? What belongs under what?

Interpretation of Data

Interpreting data and making inferences from it is essentially an inductive process of developing generalizations, although never accomplished without some application of what is previously known. This task involves four basic operations: One is that of assembling concrete information, either by instigating a process of recall and retrieval of previously learned information, or by being presented new information and identifying the specific points in this set of data. This is a basic operation and somewhat similar to the first step in grouping and classifying. Second is that of explaining or giving reasons for certain events, such as explaining why the way of life in California changed when harbors opened for free trade, or why the early colonists desired to change their form of government.

The third operation consists of relating different points of processed information, such as is involved in comparing the proportion of white population in Brazil and Argentina, and relating the information thus obtained to its possible connection with standards of living in the two countries. The fourth operation is that of formulating generalizations or inferences, such as that the countries in Latin America with predominantly white population tend to have a higher standard of living.

While these processes are generic, there are differences according to whether the content being interpreted is scientific or literary, whether the data is couched in quantitative or verbal symbols, or whether it is concrete or abstract. Greater precision is required, and fairly rigorous limits are set, for extrapolation and interpolation when interpreting quantitative data, while "reading between the lines" is almost a necessity in interpreting literary passages.[7]

---

[6] Taba and Hill (1), p. 85.

[7] Taba (2).

A graphic representation of the cognitive task of interpretation of data and the skills for using it appears below:

Interpretation of Data[8]

Overt Activity	*Covert Mental Operation*	*Eliciting Questions*
1. Identifying points	1. Differentiation	1. What did you note? see? find?
2. Explaining items of identified information	2. Relating points to each other. Determining cause and effect relationships.	2. Why did so-and-so happen?
3. Making inferences	3. Going beyond what is given. Finding implications, extrapolating.	3. What does this mean? What picture does it create in your mind? What would you conclude?

Application of Principles

A third cognitive task has to do with applying previous knowledge—principles, generalizations, or facts—to explain new phenomena and to predict consequences from known conditions. For example, if one knows what a desert is like, what way of life prevails there, and how water acts on the soil, one can predict what would happen in a desert if water were available.

Essentially, two different operations are involved: that of predicting, and that of establishing the parameters either of logical relationships or of information with which to test the validity of predictions. The level of a prediction or a hypothesis can be judged according to the extent of the leap from a given condition. But equally important is the completeness of the parameter—the chain of links which connects the prediction and the conditions. For example, the prediction that grass will grow in the desert if water is available is a prediction of a lower order than is the prediction that nomads will become farmers, and the former entails a shorter and a simpler chain of causal links.

Application of principles invites a greater degree of divergence than either of the preceding cognitive tasks. Each condition presented as data invites a divergent line of predictions. For this reason, this process contains opportunities for creative and divergent use of knowledge. In fact, some tests of creativity use situations involving prediction, but they use conditions which set few constraints and therefore permit an unlimited exercise of ingenuity.

In social situations, these processes also provoke value judgments and stereotypes. For example, in explaining why delinquency exists or in predicting how it will change if certain measures are employed, it is

[8] Taba and Hill (1), p. 94.

necessary to consider not only the factors affecting human behavior, but also what beliefs prevail about equality, justice, democratic values, deviate behavior, and adolescence.[9]

The operations involved in applying principles are quite crucial to developing productive patterns of thought. This process is the chief vehicle for transfer of knowledge. This process is, therefore, crucial for getting mileage out of the little that students can acquire directly during their schooling. It is a chief means for creating new knowledge by logical processes, and a way of acquiring control over wide areas of new phenomena. It is also the process by which models for hypothesizing can be created, freeing the individual from the necessity of being bound to the immediate stimulus.

A graphic representation of the cognitive task of application of principles and the skills for using it appears below:

Application of Principles[10]

Overt Activity	*Covert Mental Operation*	*Eliciting Questions*
1. Predicting consequences. Explaining unfamiliar phenomena. Hypothesizing.	1. Analyzing the nature of the problem or situation. Retrieving relevant knowledge.	1. What would happen if. . . .?
2. Explaining, supporting the predictions and hypotheses.	2. Determining the causal links leading to prediction or hypothesis.	2. Why do you think this would happen?
3. Verifying the prediction.	3. Using logical principles or factual knowledge to determine necessary and sufficient conditions.	3. What would it take for so-and-so to be true or probably true?

As conceptualized in the study, these three cognitive tasks have several things in common. First, the mastery of operation in each task—concept formation, interpretation, and inference and application of principles—entails a sequence of steps. For example, in order to form general concepts form diverse specific information, the operations need to be mastered in a certain sequential order: enumeration combined with differentiation → grouping, which involves determining the basis for grouping → categorizing and labeling, which involves creating superordinate classes.[11]

Despite the difference in the operations and in the specific steps, the sequences involved in mastering these steps are similar in that all involve hierarchies of levels of abstraction and complexity. Each successive step in all the cognitive tasks involves more complex operations that does the

---

[9] Taba (2).

[10] Taba and Hill (1), p. 102.

[11] Taba, Levine, and Elzey (3).

preceding one. In a sense, each step also represents an increment in the leap from that which was originally given.

Finally, the sequence of operations required in the successive steps involves different proportions of intuitive performance and of conscious awareness of the principles involved in the performance.

Indirectly, this conception of the hierarchical difficulty in levels of mental operations also involves the principle of rotation of assimilation and accommodation. This principle implies that information is at first fitted into and interpreted according to the existing conceptual system. This is followed by a type of mental activity which calls for the extension and reorganization of that conceptual system. In interpretation of data, for example, accumulation of descriptive information is followed by explanation. In the sequence involved in applying principles, the offering of intuitive and fairly unconstrained predictions or hypotheses is followed by challenging their validity by constructing the informational and logical parameters to justify them.[12]

Teaching Strategies for Cognitive Development

For the training of teachers and the design of this study, Taba evolved a paradigm of teaching in which, instead of treating teaching as a global process, specific learning tasks were defined and teaching strategies were focused on these cognitive tasks. To bring about particular behavioral changes in students, the strategies were arranged into sequential order to meet both the logical requirements of the nature of the tasks and the psychological requirements of mastering them. This means that the nature of the strategy depends on the kind of task. For example, each cognitive task (i.e., concept formation, interpretation of data, and application of principles) requires a special set of questions and a special sequencing of them. Each question is designed to elicit a special kind of overt activity, such as enumerating or explaining. This overt activity in turn fosters or requires the covert mental operation, such as differentiating in case of enumeration and seeing causal relations in case of explaining. Taba states that these covert mental operations are the ones which actually determine the sequence of learning activities and of the eliciting questions for the teacher. For example, in the task of grouping and classifying, the first question will take the form of, "What did you see, hear, note?" This calls for enumeration or listing of the items for consideration. From there the pupils must decide what belongs together. This overt activity calls for identifying a property or a characteristic that is common to all items. This characteristic becomes the basis for grouping. Finally, it is necessary to label the groups and to decide what belongs under which label.

In these operations each step is a prerequisite for the next one. One cannot label or categorize until some prior grouping has taken place, and one cannot group until the items have been listed and enumerated.

[12] *Ibid.*

For the cognitive task of interpretation of data (see chart p. 19), the overt activities are identifying points, explaining these identified items, and then making inferences or generalizations. These in turn require the covert mental operations of differentiating, explaining by comparing and contrasting, and finding implications beyond what is given. Taba suggests that a variety of learning experiences can foster this kind of cognitive task. Students may read, review audiovisual materials, observe, and do other things which furnish the data for interpreting and inferring. The learning experience must provide opportunity to differentiate the relevant from the irrelevant, to contrast and compare, to seek cause and effect relationships, and to generalize beyond what is given. This latter is difficult for many youngsters to do, because they have never been required to go beyond what is given in a book. The requirement of looking for specific answers has conditioned them against inferring from the data.

The strategy for the application of principles, the third cognitive task (see p. 20), starts with the requirement to predict consequences from described conditions. The eliciting question would be, "What would happen if . . . ?" The corresponding covert mental operation would then require the students to analyze the nature of the problem, retrieve relevant information, and use available information in order to make a valid prediction. From this point the teacher can move the pupils to the second step, explaining and supporting the prediction or hypothesis, by stating the question, "Why do you think this will happen?" This requires the students to search for causal links leading from condition to prediction. Then the final overt activity is to verify the prediction, in which case the students are required to use logical principles or factual knowledge to determine the necessary and sufficient conditions.

There is also a more or less natural placement for these tasks in the sequence of the units. Taba suggests that the beginning of the unit usually affords good opportunities for grouping and classification of information. The task of interpreting data is best performed at points at which new information, such as research, reading, or viewing of films, is gathered. The task of applying principles is usually most appropriate at the end of a unit of study, of course, after some previous knowledge has been gained and after concept formation and the interpretation of data have occurred.

Taba suggests further that the questions should be viewed as serving specific pedagogical functions. One is that of focusing. The questions should set the stage for both the kind of mental operation to be performed and the topic or the content on which this operation is to be performed. In other words, the question should tell the students what they are to talk about (such as materials used to build houses), and what they are to do with this content (whether they are to list the materials or group together materials that serve similar functions, etc.).

Another pedagogical function is that of extending thought on the same level. For example, when students are explaining events they noted in films, it is not enough for one student to give his notion. It is important to encourage others to add their ideas also. The teacher should seek additional information on already established levels of thought or elaboration and clarification of information already provided.

Finally, there is a pedagogical function of making a transition from one level of thought to another (or from one step to another), such as from assembling descriptive information to explaining certain items in that information, or from offering predictions to establishing their validity. This is a form of changing the focus, or "lifting of thought to another level."

An important consideration in all these intellectual operations is to so form the questions that the student can and will perform the operations themselves. Teachers must refrain from a temptation to offer a category, a generalization, when students have difficulty in developing one themselves. Otherwise, the students are deprived of the opportunity to learn the process. For example, in case of grouping, the students must see themselves what relationship exists between different items they have listed and devise their own categories. They must also discover that things can be grouped in different ways. An orange can be grouped with other round objects and also with the group called fruit. However, clarity of specific items is important to achieve adequate groupings, and the teacher should assist in eliciting clarification when necessary.

Naturally, the end outcomes are not perfect, especially in the first attempts. For example, the explanations of information or the generalizations and predictions may be quite defective at first, because the students have not yet mastered all the necessary processes. In time, as the work on these tasks is repeated, the responses will become more sophisticated.

An important aspect of the teaching strategy to promote autonomous performance on these cognitive tasks is that of pacing the main three questions on each task. Taba suggests that ample time should be spent on each step so that the majority of the class can participate in the practice of all three steps of each cognitive task. The class should remain on a particular step long enough to permit students who learn at different speeds to become involved and to master the needed skills.

For interpretation of data this strategy of pacing involves the following:

1. Drawing out the "what's," including questions eliciting the "who," "how," "when," and "where." The teacher must pursue these questions long enough to: (a) have the wherewithal for later comparisons, and (b) to make sure that even the slowest students are involved. If they are not included at this level of intellectual activity, they will not be able to function at subsequent levels. Where several content samples are involved, the same line of questioning must be pursued regarding each.

2. Eliciting explanations and comparisons by using questions which get at similarities, differences, changes, and the "whys." This group of questions requires the students to move to higher levels of thinking and the number of students involved at this point will be closely related to the number of students who participated at the earlier level. Dealing with these questions prepares the ground for interpretation, the making of inferences which go beyond the actual data at hand and for formulating hypotheses.

3. Probing for generalizations or consequences, which seem the likely result of selected events or series of events, by questions such as: "What does/will this mean?" Such questions set the ground for the discovery of the principles and the development of generalizations.

To summarize, pacing of the question in the sequences is all-important when the strategy involves a sequential mastery of cognitive skills where one is a prerequisite for each succeeding one. It is important also to remain at one level until a variety of responses accumulate. This case accumulation assures the availability of a wide range of information from which the students can generalize. This procedure also increases the involvement of the students, helps the majority to practice the skills, and enhances the quality of thinking at the same time.

The pacing of the transitions from one step to another radically affects the ultimate productivity of the class. Premature lifting of the thought to the next level usually brings two results: (a) fewer and fewer students participate as discussion moves on; (b) the class discussion, instead of ending on a higher level of thought, is likely to return to the most primitive level, namely, the giving of specific information.[14]

Implications for Improved Teacher Education

Professor Taba's investigation into teaching strategies for cognitive growth has many significant implications for improving the preparation of classroom teachers. Probably the most significant is the fact that her model has been developed to a point where it can be used immediately. She was able to train teachers in these skills in ten days in a public school situation. The recent development of the *Teacher Handbook for Contra Costa Social Studies, Grades 1-6* by Taba and Hill[15] brings to the reader a thorough discussion of the cognitive tasks, of the curriculum, and of the appropriate teaching strategies in the setting in which these strategies were used. A complete review of this *Handbook* should provide the teacher educator and his students some insights into the important aspects of teaching students to think. The exposition is sufficiently explicit to show the kind of curriculum organization in social studies that is needed and to give concrete guidance for designing teaching strategies for cognitive growth.

Even though this investigation was set in the social studies curriculum, Taba sees these processes as generic processes capable of being used in areas other than the social sciences, such as the "new" science and mathematics. These new curricula are presumably predicated on the same general notions. If the central concepts in these new areas are identified, the strategies for developing these concepts should be similar to those employed in the social studies. A re-analysis of the content so that the teacher can identify the basic ideas, combined with an understanding of the three basic cognitive processes, should provide for effective cognitive growth in these new curricula. These processes can be utilized at a

[14] Taba and Hill (1), p. 113.

[15] See bibliography.

secondary level also, if a knowledge of the content and an identification of the important concepts and principles are sought.

Taba assumes that three prerequisites are necessary for using her research in any curriculum area. A teacher must: (a) know the processes of thinking, (b) possess a good knowledge of the students, and (c) know the content to be taught. This demands a great deal from the teacher educator in his work with future teachers and has definite implications for the content of education courses.

Taba's investigation further emphasizes the interaction in the cognitive domain between teacher, students, and content. A careful examination of the curriculum is imperative within the framework of this research, thus pointing to the fact that teacher education students must familiarize themselves with the elements of the curriculum and the selection and use of the significant major ideas to be taught. Teacher educators should be aware of this important aspect of content selection when working with teacher education students.

Another implication important for the teacher educator to consider is that of the art of questioning. The importance of the question will be noticed from time to time throughout this entire handbook. Taba has offered some excellent suggestions within the context of her research for use in effective cognitive development. Focusing, extending, and lifting within the three major cognitive processes are important functions for the teacher. Care should be taken when working with the prospective teachers in this area. They need sufficient time and practice and must experiment with formulating open-ended questions and developing appropriate sequences during their teacher preparation work.

Professor Taba has regular sessions in which she trains teachers to utilize the various processes and strategies. Part of the training consists of experiencing the same kinds of things that school children would do. This same practice could also be employed in training new teachers: the teacher education students could learn to classify and categorize things, make inferences, and apply ideas to new problems. The introduction of such practices would require development of appropriate materials by the teacher educators. Both magnetic and video tapes that focus on definite strategies for cognitive development are beginning to be available for purposes of analysis and demonstration. Since this entire idea is a new experience for young teacher education students, a whole new frame of reference must be developed.

Finally, this entire research has significant implications for enhancing the ability of students to think. This writer will not make any judgments regarding thinking as an important goal in education. However, if one were to review current statements about goals for education, he would not find it difficult to note the central emphasis on cognitive development in the last ten years. If teacher educators want to keep abreast with this emphasis, they can find significant support from Taba's efforts for fostering the higher level of cognitive processes.

Bibliography

1. Taba, Hilda, and Hill, James J. *Teacher Handbook for Contra Costa Social Studies, Grades 1-6.* Hayward, California: Rapid Printers and Lithographers, 1965.

2. ———. *Curriculum Development: Theory and Practice.* New York: Harcourt, Brace & World, 1962.

3. ———, Levine, Samuel, and Elzey, Freeman. *Thinking in Elementary School Children.* (Cooperative Research Project No. 1574, U. S. Office of Education.) San Francisco: San Francisco State College, April 1964.

4. ———. *Teaching Strategies and Cognitive Functioning in Elementary School Children.* (Cooperative Research Project No. 2404, U. S. Office of Education.) San Francisco: San Francisco State College, 1965.

5. ———. "Teaching Strategy and Learning." *California Journal for Instructional Improvement;* December 1963.

6. ———. "The Teaching of Thinking." *Elementary English;* May 1965. pp. 534-542.

Chapter 4. Paradigms and Theories of Teaching

Professor N. L. Gage[1] has written extensively on theories, paradigms, models, and systems for teaching, learning, and research. This chapter will begin with his ideas for building paradigms and theoretical systems in the area of teaching. The discussion will then turn to his thinking on teaching, its meaning, and its analytical dimensions. A synthesis of these two areas and the implications of paradigms and theories for teaching will conclude the chapter.

To begin with, Gage states that:

> Paradigms are models, patterns, or schemata. Paradigms are not theories; they are rather ways of thinking or patterns for research that, when carried out, can lead to the development of theory.
>
> Paradigms derive their usefulness from their generality. By definition, they apply to all specific instances of a whole class of events or processes. When one has chosen a paradigm for his research, he has made crucial decisions concerning the kinds of variables and relationships between variables that he will investigate. Paradigms for research imply a kind of commitment, however preliminary or tentative, to a research program. The investigator, having chosen his paradigm, may "bite off" only a part of it for any given research project, but the paradigm of his research remains in the background, providing the framework, or sense of the whole, in which his project is embedded.
>
> A second characteristic of paradigms is that they often represent variables and their relationships in some graphic or outline form. Events or phenomena that have various temporal, spatial, causal, or logical relationships are portrayed in these relationships by boxes, connecting lines, and positions on vertical and horizontal dimensions. The classical portrayal of Pavlovian conditioning, shown in Fig. 1, illustrates this aspect of a paradigm. The left-hand part of Fig. 1 shows an unconditioned stimulus, S_1, eliciting a response, R. The center part

[1] Dr. Gage is Professor of Education and Psychology at Stanford University and Co-Director of the Stanford Center for Research and Development in Teaching.

shows S_1 being regularly preceded by another stimulus, S_2. Eventually, as shown in the right-hand part, S_2 alone becomes able to elicit R.

Figure 1. A Paradigm for Pavlovian Conditioning.

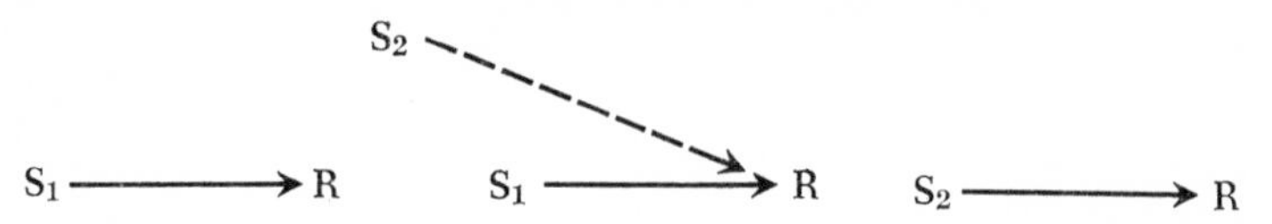

Here, the paradigm's generality implies that the process will occur regardless of the particular kinds of stimuli and responses involved. The stimuli may be bells, food powder, lights, words, electric shocks, the sight of people, an approving "uh-huh" expression, or whatever; the response may be salivation, muscle movement, increased heartbeat, use of the word "I," favorable self-references, or whatever. The paradigm is intended to be general and apply to all of the possibilities. It can serve research by suggesting that various specific instances of the general classes S_1, S_2 and R be tried. Also, various temporal relations between S_1 and S_2 can be explored; thus, the question can be raised whether S_2 must always precede S_1, and whether the interval between S_1 and S_2 affects the conditioning process. In this paradigm, the horizontal (left-right) dimension is a temporal one.[2]

Regarding their effectiveness Gage further states that:

Paradigms, like theories, can be either explicit or implicit. Some have been set forth by their authors in full panoply, with diagrams and elaborations of their connections with completed or projected research. Other paradigms are implicit in what authors have done or proposed by way of research; in these cases, we shall seek to use the paradigm as an intellectual tool for examining crucial aspects of research on teaching.

Choice of a paradigm, whether deliberate or unthinking, determines much about the research that will be done. The style, design, and approach of a research undertaking, indeed, the likelihood that it will bear fruit, are conditioned in large part by the paradigm with which the investigator begins. Whether he will perform an experiment, in the sense of actually manipulating one or more variables, or a correlational study, in the sense of studying relationships between variables measured as they occur in nature, may be determined by his paradigm.

Whether he will seek relationships between variables that have some genuine promise, based on logical and empirical grounds, of being related, may be determined by his paradigm. At one extreme, his paradigm may lead him to search for relationships between variables that have a good likelihood of being related. So one investigation may examine the correlation between the teacher's authoritarianism on a verbal, printed test, and the teacher's likelihood of non-promoting students, because a paradigm (implicit in this case) portrays a connection between these variables; in one investigation the results supported the hypothesis and the paradigm was strengthened. At the other extreme, the paradigm may lead inevitably to negative results. Thus a paradigm may lead to an investigation of the correlation between the teacher's authoritarianism and his effectiveness in producing gain in reading achievement; explication of the paradigm underlying this project might suggest in advance the forlornness of any hope that such a relationship will materialize.[3]

In the above discussion, it can be seen that paradigms must be general,

[2] Gage (1), pp. 95-96.
[3] *Ibid.*, p. 96.

can be either explicit or implicit, and must indicate the relationship between the variables. Further, the paradigm should show how the variables react on one another and indicate what is important in a person's schemata of something. Only after considerable testing and verification can a model or paradigm advance to the theory stage.

In regard to the second half of the title of this chapter, Gage suggests that the single term "teaching" can be quite misleading, if it is taken to imply that a single theory can cover a wide variety of teacher activities. There is, therefore, no such thing as a single theory or model for all aspects of teaching. It must be broken down into smaller models, such as teaching for cognitive development or teaching for conditioning (the obverse of the corresponding conceptions of learning). At this time, there is no meta-theory of teaching which puts all of its aspects and forms together into a grand model. Since paradigms are necessary for the development of theories, and since theories are important for analysis and for trial purposes, Gage offers some guides to what is necessary for such development. His illustrative analysis of teaching[4] may assist educators in the development of paradigms for classroom work.

Gage first suggests that *types of teaching activities* have a bearing on the development of appropriate models for teaching. The kind of activity the teacher engages in—explaining, guiding, making assignments, etc.—must be specified. Gage feels that one model or theory cannot encompass all of these activities.

Gage next identifies *educational goals* as an important facet of teaching. Does teaching take the same form for cognitive, affective, and psychomotor objectives? Would one process or model cover all of these goals? Gage again argues that no one model or theory would apply to the development of thinking, attitudes, interests, physical abilities, etc.

The third analysis for consideration would be that according to what Gage terms *components of teaching corresponding to those of learning*. This analysis refers to a mirror image of the learning process and involves such things as motivation-producing, cue-providing, response-eliciting, and reinforcement-providing. Again, all of these aspects of teaching cannot be subsumed under one model for the teaching act, because, for instance, motivation-producing entails different activities and variables from reinforcement-providing.

The fourth analysis for the analysis of teaching suggested by Gage *derives from kinds of learning theory*. Illustrations of these kinds of theory would be conditioning theory, identification theory, and cognitive theory. Different kinds may be appropriate for different kinds of teaching in different situations, and expecting them to yield a single theory on teaching, argues Gage, would be inappropriate. A unified model should not be sought, because cognitive restructuring involves different views of teaching from either identification or conditioning, and so forth.

---

[4] Gage (3); for another excellent paper on research on the cognitive aspects of teaching, see Gage (4).

These four analyses imply that "no single theory of teaching should be offered that would attempt to account for all activities of teachers, that would be aimed at all objectives of education, that would involve all components of the learning process, in a way that would satisfy all theories of learning."[5]

From these analyses, in what direction should the educator go? Gage suggests that one can draw upon various resultants of these analyses and combine them to form a model for development, testing, and analysis. In other words, the teaching activity depends on the nature of the educational goal selected. From this selection one would move to the appropriate component of the learning process and then to the theory of learning that would best accomplish the particular objective. Each phase of the paradigm must fit each other one.

Gage offers several examples of such selections. These selections lead to paradigms on which we can base theoretical formulations of teaching. In the first example, the activity of explaining is selected from among possible teaching activities. Next, the cognitive objective of "ability to extrapolate" is chosen as the desired outcome or goal. The component of the learning process in this case would be a perceptual one, and the teacher would, in turn, direct the student's perception to the important part of the task. The theory of learning would in this case be that of cognitive restructuring. These choices of elements seem to be consistent, to fulfill the stated objectives, and to suggest a theoretical framework ready for analysis and testing. Gage suggests that, in this example, the most arguable element would be the cognitive restructuring model. Upon analysis, however, the conditioning and identification models would have to be rejected, since the cognitive task of extrapolation makes the restructuring of the cognitive configuration seem necessary. Imitation or conditioning seems less appropriate to the goal of ability to extrapolate.

In another case, the teaching function would be mental hygiene, the affective goal would be emotional security in the classroom, the component of learning process would be motivation, and the family of learning theory would be conditioning. These could form another defensible model for effective teaching. In this case, the teacher can motivate the student toward positive attitudes, reward and praise him for his acts, and reinforce his behavior when necessary. With this kind of teaching activity, the student can begin to develop a more secure feeling. The conditioning model is used here because there is no logical cognitive structure for this kind of behavior and thus no rational explanation or intellectual argument. The identification approach would likewise be rejected, because the teacher does not want the student to behave like him: a student cannot effectively imitate the emotional security of the teacher.

A final example might consist in the specifications for teaching handwriting, an objective in the psychomotor domain. The response component of the learning process and the imitation conception of learning

[5] Gage (3), p. 277.

would complete the specification of this act of teaching. The student would achieve the psychomotor objective of learning to write capital or small letters by responding to the teacher and actually imitating the teacher's behavior. Since almost no rational grounds are involved in this activity, one could not build a case for learning based on cognitive restructuring. Also, the conditioning model could be rejected because the lengthy task of shaping through trial-response and reinforcement would be too time-consuming for his psychomotor goal. The imitation of the prestigious model suffices in this case.

In these three cases, it can be seen that each teaching task requires different specifications of elements and thus different models and theoretical formulations. Gage concedes that a variety of combinations might be devised and then analyzed to determine their applicability to a teaching situation.

Implications for Improved Teacher Education

Gage sees a need for some structuring of the teaching function. Theoretical analyses of teaching are as important as theories of learning and should be developed alongside learning theories rather than inferred from them. The emphasis again is on theories (plural) because no single, unified theory can encompass the varieties of elements analyzed and described by Gage. And of course, before validated theory can be achieved, paradigms must be developed and tested.

Since models of many aspects of teaching are lacking, more development of models is necessary. This development can make explicit some internally consistent specifications in a model and test them. When models appear to be useful, ways of implementing them may be sought. The development of paradigms helps to form a conception of what elements are important and what relationships exist among these elements. A careful examination of the elements of teaching, a review of pertinent data from other sources, and the testing of existing models (highly endorsed by Gage) would be the starting points for paradigm development and testing.

Bibliography

1. Gage, N. L. "Paradigms for Research on Teaching." *Handbook of Research on Teaching*. Chicago: Rand McNally & Co., 1963. Chapter 3, pp. 94-141.
2. ———. "This Side of Paradigms: The State of Research on Teaching English." National Council of Teachers of English. Proceedings of the San Francisco Conference. The Council, 1963.
3. ———. "Theories of Teaching." *Theories of Learning and Instruction, 63rd Yearbook*. National Society for the Study of Education. Chicago: The Society, 1964. pp. 268-285.
4. ———. "Research on Cognitive Aspects of Teaching." *The Way Teaching Is*. Washington, D. C.: Association for Supervision and Curriculum Development and the National Education Association, 1966. pp. 29-44.
5. ———. "Toward a Cognitive Theory of Teaching." *Teachers College Record* 65: 408-412; February 1964.

Chapter 5. Interaction Analysis

Professor Ned Flanders[1] and associates through extensive investigation and development have effected a system for ascertaining the student-teacher verbal interaction in a classroom. This system, called "Interaction Analysis," could be defined as the systematic quantification of behavioral acts or qualities of behavior acts as they occur in some sort of spontaneous interaction. This chapter will focus its attention on the system, its use and meaning, and on the significant implications that it possesses for the improvement of teacher education at the preservice level.

The Flanders system was developed as part of some extensive research into teacher influence and pupil attitudes and achievement. As a result of these investigations, Flanders suggested that teacher influence could be analyzed within the context of verbal behavior of both the teacher and student. Verbal behavior is utilized here primarily because it can be observed with higher reliability than can nonverbal behavior, with the assumption that the verbal behavior of an individual is an adequate sample of his total behavior. Within the major area of verbal behavior in a classroom is, of course, the talking by the teacher and that by the students. To ascertain, then, the true interaction in verbal behavior in a classroom, both teacher talk and student talk should be measured and described. Within the larger category of teacher talk, Flanders has sought to determine the teacher influence factor, or the amount of freedom the teacher grants to the student. Direct influence, the first factor as Flanders sees it, tends to minimize the freedom of the student, because the teacher directs the learning activity. The second factor, indirect influence, would have the opposite effect, or that of maximizing the freedom of the student to respond. The teacher talk area of indirect and direct influence is further divided into seven specific categories. The student talk is divided into two specific categories. Rounding out the ten-category system is that of silence or confusion where no significant verbal behavior is found.

[1] Dr. Flanders is Professor of Education at the University of Michigan.

Flanders identified the ten-category system as follows: (a) accepting student feelings, (b) giving praise, (c) accepting, clarifying, or making use of a student's ideas, (d) asking a question, (e) lecturing, giving facts or opinions, (f) giving directions, (g) giving criticism, (h) student response, (i) student initiation, and (j) confusion or silence. The first seven are assigned to teacher talk.

A description of the categories in the Flanders system for interaction analysis is as follows:

CATEGORIES FOR VERBAL INTERACTION IN THE CLASSROOM

Indirect Teacher Behavior

Category 1, Acceptance of Feeling. The teacher accepts feelings when he says he understands how the children feel, that they have the right to have these feelings, and that he will not punish the children for their feelings. These kinds of statements often communicate to children both acceptance and clarification of the feeling.

Also included in this category are statements that recall past feeling, refer to enjoyable or uncomfortable feelings that are present, or predict happy or sad events that will occur in the future.

In our society people often react to expressions of negative feelings by offering negative feelings in return. Acceptance of these emotions in the classroom is quite rare; probably because teachers find it difficult to accept negative emotional behavior. However, it may be just as difficult for them to accept positive feelings. Feelings expressed by students may also be ignored by the teacher if he considers the classroom to be a place where people are concerned primarily with ideas rather than feelings.

Category 2, Praise or Encouragement. Included in this category are jokes that release tension, but not those that threaten students or are made at the expense of individual students. Often praise is a single word: "good," "fine," or "right." Sometimes the teacher simply says, "I like what you are doing." Encouragement is slightly different and includes statements such as, "Continue." "Go ahead with what you are saying." "Uh huh; go on; tell us more about your idea."

Category 3, Accepting Ideas. This category is quite similar to Category 1; however, it includes only acceptance of student ideas, not acceptance of expressed emotion. When a student makes a suggestion, the teacher may paraphrase the student's statement, restate the idea more simply, or summarize what the student has said. The teacher may also say, "Well, that's an interesting point of view. I see what you mean." Statements belonging in Category 3 are particularly difficult to recognize; often the teacher will shift from using the student's idea to stating the teacher's own idea.

Statements belonging in Category 3 can be identified by asking the question, "Is the idea that the teacher is now stating the student's or is it the teacher's?" If it is the student's idea, then this category is used; if it is the teacher's, another category must be employed.

Category 4, Asking Questions. This category includes only questions to which the teacher expects an answer from the pupils. If a teacher asks a question and then follows it immediately with a statement of opinion, or if he begins lecturing, obviously the question was not meant to be answered. A rhetorical question is not categorized as a question. An example of another kind of question that should not be classified in Category 4 is the following: "What in the world do you think you are doing out of your seat, John?" With proper intonation the question is designed to get John back in his seat; if such is the case, it must be categorized as criticism of the student's behavior (Category 7).

Questions that are meant to be answered are of several kinds. There are questions that are direct in the sense that there is a right and wrong answer. The question, "What are 2 and 2?" is a question that limits the freedom of the student to some extent. Although he can refuse to answer, give the wrong answer, or make a statement of another kind, in general, this kind of question focuses the student's answer more than does a question such as, "What do you think we ought to do now?" Questions, then, can be either narrow and restrict the student in his answer, or they can be very broad and give the student a great deal of freedom in answering. All questions, however broad or narrow, which require answers and are not commands or criticism, fall into Category 4.

Direct Teacher Behavior

Category 5, Lecture. Lecture is the form of verbal interaction that is used to give information, facts, opinions, or ideas to children. The presentation of material may be used to introduce, review, or focus the attention of the class on an important topic. Usually information in the form of lecture is given in fairly extended time periods, but it may be interspersed with children's comments, questions, and encouraging praise.

Whenever the teacher is explaining, discussing, giving opinion, or giving facts or information, Category 5 is used. Rhetorical questions are also included in this category. Category 5 is the one most frequently used in classroom observation.

Category 6, Giving Directions. The decision about whether or not to clas-sifiy the statement as a direction or command must be based on the degree of freedom that the student has in response to teacher direction. When the teacher says, "Will all of you stand up and stretch?" he is obviously giving a direction. If he say, "John, go to the board and write your name," he is giving a direction or command. When he says, "John, I want you to tell me what you have done with your reader," he is still giving a direction.

Category 7, Criticizing or Justifying Authority. A statement of criticism is one that is designed to change student behavior from nonacceptable to acceptable. The teacher is saying, in effect, "I don't like what you are doing. Do something else." Another group of statements included in this category are those that might be called statements of defense or self-justification. These statements are particularly difficult to detect when a teacher appears to be explaining a lesson or the reasons for doing a lesson to the class. If the teacher is explaining himself or his authority, defending himself against the student, or justifying himself, the statement falls in this category. Other kinds of statements that fall in this category are those of extreme self-reference or those in which the teacher is constantly asking the children to do something as a special favor to the teacher.

Categories 1 through 4, those of indirect teacher influence, and Categories 5 through 7, those of direct teacher influence, have been described. They are all categories of teacher talk. Whenever the teacher is talking, the statements must be categorized in one of the first seven categories. If the observer decides that with a given statement the teacher is restricting the freedom of children, the statement is tallied in Categories 5, 6, or 7. If, on the other hand, the observer decides that the teacher is expanding freedom of children, the category used is either 1, 2, 3, or 4. There are three additional categories for use in classroom interaction:

Category 8, Student Talk-Response. This category is used when the teacher has initiated the contact or has solicited student statements, when the student answers a question asked by the teacher or when he responds verbally to a direction the teacher has given. Anything that the student says that is clearly in response to initiation by the teacher belongs in Category 8.

Category 9, Student Talk-Initiation. In general, if the student raises his hand to make a statement or to ask a question when he has not been prompted to do so by the teacher, the appropriate category is nine.

Distinguishing between Categories 8 and 9 is often difficult. Predicting the general kind of answer that the student will give in response to a question from the teacher is important in making this distinction. If the answer is one that is of a type predicted by the observer (as well as the teacher and class), then the statement comes under Category 8. When in response to a teacher-question the student gives an answer different from that which is expected for that particular question, then the statement is categorized as a nine.

Category 10, Silence or Confusion. This category includes anything else not included in the other categories. Periods of confusion in communication, when it is difficult to determine who is talking, are classified in this category.[2]

A summary of these categories, with brief definitions for use of the observer follows.

Summary of Categories for Interaction Analysis[3]

TEACHER TALK	INDIRECT INFLUENCE	1. *ACCEPTS FEELING: accepts and clarifies the feeling tone of the students in a non-threatening manner. Feelings may be positive or negative. Predicting and recalling feelings are included.
		2. *PRAISES OR ENCOURAGES: praises or encourages student action or behavior. Jokes that release tension, not at the expense of another individual, nodding head or saying "uh huh?" or "go on" are included.
		3. *ACCEPTS OR USES IDEAS OF STUDENT: clarifying, building, or developing ideas or suggestions by a student. As teacher brings more of his own ideas into play, shift to category five.
		4. *ASKS QUESTIONS: asking a question about content or procedure with the intent that a student answer.
	DIRECT INFLUENCE	5. *LECTURES: giving facts or opinions about content or procedure; expressing his own idea; asking rhetorical questions.
		6. *GIVES DIRECTIONS: directions, commands, or orders with which a student is expected to comply.
		7. *CRITICIZES OR JUSTIFIES AUTHORITY: statements intended to change student behavior from nonacceptable to acceptable pattern; bawling someone out; stating why the teacher is doing what he is doing, extreme self-reference.

* There is no scale implied by these numbers. Each number is classificatory; it designates a particular kind of communication event. To write these numbers down during observation is to enumerate, not to judge, a position on a scale.

[2] Amidon and Flanders (1), pp. 6-11.

[3] Flanders (3), p. 3.

(Continued on next page.)

Summary of Categories for Interaction Analysis (Continued)

STUDENT TALK	8. *STUDENT TALK-RESPONSE: talk by students in response to teacher. Teacher initiates the contact or solicits student statement. 9. *STUDENT TALK-INITIATION: talk by students, which they initiate. If "calling on" student is only to indicate who may talk next, observer must decide whether student wanted to talk. If he did, use this category.
	10. *SILENCE OR CONFUSION: pauses, short periods of silence, and periods of confusion in which communication cannot be understood by the observer.

To use[4] this system for analysis purposes requires an observer who has had some training in and adequate knowledge of the categories. The observer marks the appropriate category of behavior as the teacher teaches. There are actually two ways to record verbal interaction in the classroom. One way would be to simply record (with a mark) the occurrences in one of the ten categories. An example would look something like this:

The verbal interaction in a science classroom might go something like this: First of all silence (10); then a directive of, "Take out your books" (6); "Open them to page 27" (6); some confusion (10); then the teacher asks, "What did you think about this chapter?" (4); a student responds, "It was interesting" (8); another student states, however, "I didn't understand the first part" (9); "What didn't you understand?" (4); "I'm not sure that I understand the experiment" (8); "Did others of you understand the experiment?" (4); one student says, "Yes" (8); the teacher says, "Can you explain it to the class?" (4); the student explains the experiment (8); the teacher says, "That's very good" (2); but since the student left out some important facts, the teacher explains more completely the experiment (5). The final marking of the tallies in the category system would look something like this:

1	2	3	4	5	6	7	8	9	10
	1		1111	1	11		1111	1	11

This system shows where the teacher concentrates his efforts.

* There is no scale implied by these numbers. Each number is classificatory; it designates a particular kind of communication event. To write these numbers down during observation is to enumerate, not to judge, a position on a scale.

[4] For a more comprehensive discussion on using this system, see Amidon and Flanders (1).

The second method would be to record the appropriate category number as it is observed and place all numbers in sequence one after another. An example of this kind of observation method, using the verbal discourse from the above example, would look like this:

10	8	
6	4	
6	8	
10	4	
4	8	
8	2	
9	5	
4	10	(always ends with 10; see below)

Of course, both methods of recording verbal behavior have their purposes, but the second can reveal more pertinent data about the moves and their sequence. This is more significant for analysis and corrective purposes and is recommended for the observers.

To get an adequate sample of interaction, Flanders suggests that a mark for recording a number should be made every three seconds, which will record twenty instances in a minute. During a recorded period of a class session there will be several columns of numbers. It is important that the tempo be kept as steady as possible and that the observer be as accurate as possible. He may also wish to jot down marginal notes from time to time, which can later assist in the explanation of what happened in the classroom. Flanders further suggests that the observer-recorder should orient himself to the classroom situation for about ten minutes before he begins his categorizing. This short time will permit the observer to get a feeling for the kind of activities that will transpire.

When the activity of the classroom changes, the observer should note this. For example, a class discussion on a topic may stop with some directions by the teacher, then the students may form small groups for independent discussion. Finally, the observer should note the kind of class activity that is taking place. A review of some subject matter topic will reveal considerably different data than an introduction to a new topic by the teacher. The teacher-pupil interaction will be different in different situations even when directed by the same teacher.

Some ground rules that may assist the recorder of interaction are as follows:

Ground Rules

Rule 1: When not certain in which of two or more categories a statement belongs, choose the category that is numerically farthest from Category 5, except 10.

Rule 2: If the primary tone of the teacher's behavior has been consistently direct or consistently indirect, do not shift into the opposite classification unless a clear indication of shift is given by the teacher.

Rule 3: The observer must not be overly concerned with his own biases or with the teacher's intent.

Rule 4: If more than one category occurs during the three-second interval, then all categories used in the interval are recorded; therefore, record each change in category. If no change occurs within three seconds, repeat that category number.

Rule 5: If a silence is long enough for a break in the interaction to be discernible, and if it occurs at a three-second recording time, it is recorded as a 10.[5]

As suggested above, the recording of interaction data in sequence is important for the analysis process. Once it has been recorded, an interpretation may begin. The process for analyzing the sequence of events can be accomplished by placing the numbers on a matrix or a ten-row by ten-column table. The matrix (see example below) permits the teacher to examine the kinds of interactions that have taken place during his teaching.

For placing the data on the matrix, the numbers must be paired. The first number of the pair is concerned with the row and the second number is concerned with the column. The second number of the pair becomes the first number of the new pair. Each pair of numbers overlaps with the previous pair and each number is used twice, with the exception of the first and last. The first and last numbers should always be ten to make analysis easier and because it can be assumed that any session starts with silence and ends the same way. To illustrate the pairing of numbers, some examples may help.[6] Suppose the sequencing of numbers were as follows:

Sequence		Pairing
10		10)
6		(6)
10		(10)
7		(7)
6		(6)
1		(1)
1		(1)
4	The pairing would thus be	(4)
8		(8)
8		(8)
8		(8)
2		(2)
3		(3)
3		(3)
10		(10

The pairing of numbers, then, assists the person to place the pairs in the appropriate cell of the matrix. The first number dictates the row; the second the column. Placing the above fifteen numbers in proper pairs would result in this kind of matrix:

[5] Amidon and Flanders (1).

[6] Amidon and Flanders (1), p. 26.

Sample Interaction Matrix[7]

Second

Columns

First ROWS

	1	2	3	4	5	6	7	8	9	10	
1	1			1							
2			1								
3			1							1	
4								1			
5											
6	1									1	
7						1					
8		1						11			
9											
10						1	1				
Total	2	1	2	1	0	2	1	3	0	2	14

The matrix records only fourteen tallies, or one less than the original tally of fifteen, and it can be checked by comparing the numbers in each row with the numbers in each column. If the numbers are equal, the matrix is correctly tabulated. It should be noted that it is advisable to develop a separate matrix for each lesson and large activity. In doing this a comparison of lessons is possible.

Once the matrix is completed with the verbal interaction data, the analysis process can begin. There are a variety of directions that the analyst can go from this point, and it would depend, of course, on the original purpose of the lesson or activity. Flanders stresses the identification of purpose for the teaching activity, because besides being important for teaching, the analysis will then check to see if the goal was met. In other words, if the teacher were to present content only, he would conduct the learning activity in a different fashion than if he wanted to encourage class discussion on an important area of interest to the students.

One thing the analyst could do before any other activity would be to determine the percentage of time spent in each cell. This is done by dividing 100 by the total marks on the matrix and using the quotient to

[7] Amidon and Flanders (1), p. 27.

multiply the total for each column. Further, teacher talk (columns 1-7) and student talk (columns 8 and 9) can be determined by adding the appropriate column percentages. And finally, the analyst can determine the ratio of indirect influence of teacher talk (columns 1-4) to the direct influence of teacher talk (columns 5, 6, 7) by dividing the first total by the second. All of this basic data is important for the teacher to view in terms of classroom verbal interaction.

From this point the teacher-analyst may look for other specific aspects of his classroom interaction. Some brief examples are:

A heavy loading of both the 4 and 5 rows and columns indicates emphasis on content, because these cells consist primarily of lectures, statements of opinion, and teacher questions about information and content.

A pattern of 6-6, 6-7, 7-6, 7-7 often indicates discipline problems or problems of student rejection of teacher influence. High, direct influence can be seen from a heavy loading of these cells.

Indirect influence can be easily ascertained by viewing the 1-1, 1-2, 1-3, 2-1, 2-2, 2-3, 3-1, 3-2, and 3-3 cells. In this case the teacher has accepted and extended student ideas and statements and has enlarged upon student feelings.

The important function of teacher responses to student comment can be checked by viewing the 8 and 9 rows of a matrix. A heavy loading of columns 1 and 4 in these rows indicates that the teacher is using an indirect approach, and columns 5, 6, 7 in these rows show a direct response to student comments.

The above are but a few of the many interpretations that can result from an analysis of the matrix. Once the observer gains a working knowledge of the interaction system he can ascertain all kinds of meaningful patterns from the matrix. And when the data and patterns of interaction are determined, the teacher can make the appropriate changes in his behavior to more closely accomplish his stated purpose. This can be done with practice on questioning, involving students, and a variety of other techniques. Finally, the system can be used again until the actual verbal behavior comes as close to the stated purpose as possible.

Implications for Improved Teacher Education

The Flanders system of interaction analysis has many far-reaching implications for the teacher education process. First of all, the system is highly developed and has been used quite extensively. Flanders and associates have collected considerable data with this system for research purposes[8] as well as determining the verbal behavior in the classroom for improvement purposes.

Second, the system is an analytical tool for describing and analyzing the kinds of verbal interaction that take place between the teacher and his

[8] For review of research, see bibliography at end.

students. To those who subscribe to an analytical approach to the teaching-learning process, this system would be most applicable. Although it has its limitations, it can deliver important data to the teacher for his analysis and improvement. Since the meaning of this highly developed tool for determining verbal interaction in a classroom is perhaps readily apparent to the teacher educator, some attention should be given to its use for and in programs of teacher education.

Flanders suggests that there are perhaps two approaches to introducing this system to teacher education students. One would be to simply give this system to the students and let them learn about it themselves, and the second would be a more gradual approach.

In the first case, the students could learn about the system from the manual or some other source. They could learn the categories, understand the meaning of each, and begin to do some simple recording of data. In time the students could become accomplished in the process of recording data. Then the introduction to the use of the matrix and the analysis process would follow. New patterns of verbal interaction could be tried by the students in their work. Recording of the interaction could occur in a public or laboratory school or in simulated (or role-playing) or laboratory sessions in the college. Analysis of data could then be done by the students with the instructor or in groups. Flanders reports that interest runs high with preservice students when they use and interpret the system.

In the second case, students could start on a more limited basis where only two or three categories would be used. These categories could be defined by the students themselves or cooperatively with the instructor, and might include such items as: Does the teacher accept the ideas of the students, does he encourage the students to ask questions, and does he ask questions himself? Another limited system might be: Does he lecture, does he give directions, and does he criticize? Another category of "none of the above" should be added so that the remainder of the interaction can be recorded. This last category makes it possible to give some statistical significance to the recording session, because all time spent observing will be recorded on the tally sheet. Because of this the student can determine the time spent criticizing, praising, asking questions, etc. Once the students have the feel for this analysis process, they can move to other categories, and finally to the Flanders system. This approach may be more appropriate, because it works with the concern of students for important things in a classroom activity. The gradual move to a more sophisticated analysis may come easier for the students.

In either approach, starting with just tallies is sufficient at first. Then figuring the percentage of time spent in each category would follow before the actual sequencing of numbers and the matrix work.

Flanders suggests that the three-second rule be waived in the beginning as long as a constant tempo set by the students is maintained. The use of the three-second recording rule will come with time, and it should not be pushed at the beginning.

Flanders' system can be expanded or modified to ascertain other kinds of verbal behavior in the classroom. Subscripts within the present system are possible where one, for example, might look at the kinds of questions that are being asked in Category 4. Or, perhaps, one might try to break down Category 6 to look at the nature of the directions that a classroom teacher gives. Also, a new category system may be developed to check completely different processes. Flanders suggests that Taba's cognitive tasks (Chapter 3) might be placed in a category system for classroom checking. Flanders has mentioned that he knows of about twenty-five category systems that have been developed from his original system, with one having forty-four different categories. So the modification of Flanders' basic system can offer the teacher educator and his students some significant and flexible possibilities. The only requirements in this case are the establishment of purposes and creative thought and development.

A final requirement strongly emphasized by Professor Flanders for the use of the Interaction Analysis System, whether it may be in a methods course, student teaching, an introduction to education course, or a newer theory and analysis of teaching course, is that of a free and assuring, give-and-take atmosphere. To use Flanders' system means quite obviously that someone must teach while someone observes and records (unless, of course, a tape recorder is used). To assess the verbal behavior of a person working with students in a classroom situation could be a threatening situation if the proper attitude did not exist. The positive atmosphere of inquiry, investigation, and growth must prevail in such a situation, and the teacher education instructor is the key to the establishment of such a feeling. He should probably experience this interaction process before working with his students so that he can view the analysis and criticism involved. This could be done with a tape recorded session of his own teaching. Then he could teach perhaps one brief lesson in three different ways and have the students observe and record. At this point an open analysis and criticism could occur, with students and instructor cooperatively performing this function.

Then the instructor may re-teach with different, prescribed moves so the analysis may be done again. With the instructor serving as the guinea pig in the analysis work, the students will begin to see the meaning of the analytical and growth process in a truly professional atmosphere. The establishment of this attitude and the development of an analytical behavior are in themselves significant reasons for incorporating Flanders' *Interaction Analysis* in teacher education course work.

Bibliography

1. Amidon, Edmund J. and Flanders, Ned A. *The Role of the Teacher in the Classroom: A Manual for Understanding and Improving Teachers' Classroom Behavior.* Minneapolis: Paul S. Amidon and Associates, 1963.

2. Flanders, Ned A. "Intent, Action, and Feedback: A Preparation for Teachers." *Journal of Teacher Education,* pp. 251-260; September 1963.

3. ———. "Interaction Analysis: A Technique for Quantifying Teacher Influence." Paper presented at the American Educational Research Association Conference, February 1961.

4. ———. "Some Relationships Among Teacher Influence, Pupil Attitudes and Achievement." *Contemporary Research on Teacher Effectiveness.* Edited by Bruce J. Biddle and William J. Ellena. New York: Holt, Rinehart & Winston, 1964. Chapter 7, pp. 196-231.

5. ———. "Teacher Influence in the Classroom: I. Research on Classroom Climate." *Theory and Research in Teaching.* Edited by A. A. Bellack. New York: Teachers College, Columbia University, 1963. pp. 37-53.

6. ———. "Teacher Influence-Pupil Attitudes and Achievement." Final Report. (Cooperative Research Project No. 397, U. S. Department of Health, Education and Welfare, Office of Education.) University of Minnesota, 1960.

7. ———. "Using Interaction Analysis in the Inservice Training of Teachers." *Journal of Experimental Education,* pp. 313-316; September 1963.

Chapter 6. The Language of the Classroom

Professor Arno Bellack[1] and associates conducted an extensive, empirical, and descriptive study into the linguistic behavior of teachers and students in fifteen social studies classrooms in the metropolitan New York City area. This chapter will describe the nature, some of the pertinent results, and the meaning of the study for improved teacher education.

Professor Bellack felt that, before any prescriptive work on the teaching act could be done, there must be a description of just what occurs in a classroom. Further, the nature of the classroom activities of both students and teachers is such that a large measure of what happens transpires through the verbal interaction of both parties. Verbal interaction, in this case, means the communication of language and meaning in the classroom, which in turn tends to indicate the behavior of those involved in the classroom. Few classroom activities, it was argued, can be carried on in the absence of language. Thus, this study focused on the systematic analysis of the linguistic events in the classroom. This study took place under the assumption that the primary function of language is the communication of meaning, and that describing linguistic events in the classroom in terms of the meanings expressed by teachers and students was a meaningful direction for study.

In this case, Bellack drew from Wittgenstein[2] the notion that the meaning of a word is its use in the language; thus, the identification of the distinctive functions language actually serves in verbal interplay and the meanings that are conveyed through words is the essential direction in the study of teaching.

In this search for the meaning of communication in the classroom by teachers and students, Bellack identified three major areas for investigation: (a) What was the speaker doing pedagogically, (b) what was the content

[1] Dr. Bellack is Professor of Education at Teachers College, Columbia University.

[2] Wittgenstein, Ludwig. *Philosophical Investigations*. Oxford: Basil Blackwell, 1958.

of his statement, and (c) what was the emotional meaning or feeling tone in the communication. In other words, the pedagogical significance of the utterences (giving directions, asking or answering questions) of the speakers, the particular content that was being communicated, and the explicit and implicit emotional vocal expression of the speakers were the important dimensions of meaning communicated in the classroom, and thus were recorded and analyzed by Bellack.

In the operational definition of the means for measuring and describing the linguistic events in the classroom, Bellack's work was again influenced by the work of Wittgenstein,[3] in which certain roles are expected to be played in use of language. Wittgenstein identified various types of activities that are linguistic in nature and termed them "language games" because these "activities assume different forms and structures according to the function they come to serve in different contexts."[4] There are a definite structure and certain moves that a player makes as he plays a game. The role of linguistic behavior follows like a game in the classroom, because students and teachers play certain roles or are guided by certain conventions according to the learning activity.

Bellack saw the language game idea fitting into the study of teaching, because teaching is like a game in that it is a form of social activity whereby teachers and students play complementary roles in the classroom, and there are certain ground rules which guide the actions of teachers and students in their activities. The reasoning then followed that, if the research could identify the verbal moves that were made in the classroom "game" and the rules by which teachers and students were playing, the functions of the verbal actions and the meanings that are communicated could be determined.

From this point on, the verbal actions or pedagogical moves could be determined in terms of what teaching function they perform in the classroom. Four major categories of pedagogical moves were defined. They are as follows:

> *Structuring.* Structuring moves serve the pedagogical functions of focusing attention on subject matter or classroom procedures and launching interaction between students and teachers. They set the context for subsequent behavior or performance. For example, teachers frequently begin a class period with a structuring move in which they focus attention on the topic or problem to be discussed during that session.
>
> *Soliciting.* Moves in this category are designed to elicit a verbal response, encourage persons addressed to attend to something, or elicit a physical response. All genuine questions are solicitations, as are commands, imperatives, and requests.
>
> *Responding.* These moves bear a reciprocal relationship to soliciting moves and occur only in relation to them. Their pedagogical function is to fulfill the expectation of soliciting moves. Thus, students' answers to teachers' questions are classified as responding moves.
>
> *Reacting.* These moves are occasioned by a structuring, soliciting, respond-

[3] *Ibid.*

[4] Bellack, *et al.* (2), pp.4-5.

ing, or another reacting move, but are not directly elicited by them. Pedagogically, these moves serve to shape or mold classroom discourse by accepting, rejecting, modifying, or expanding what has been said previously. Reacting moves differ from responding moves, in that while a responding move is always directly elicited by a solicitation, preceding moves serve only as the occasion for reactions. Evalution by a teacher of a student's response, for example, is designated a reacting move.[5]

From the analysis of the data in the pedagogical moves mentioned above, Bellack was able to discern some patterns or moves which were designated as teaching cycles. The cycle began with either a structuring move or a soliciting move, which Bellack termed initiating maneuvers. These maneuvers served to get the cycle under way. The types of maneuvers that are termed reflexive covered the responding and reacting moves in the teaching cycle and thus completed the cycles. The typical cycle may begin with a question, which is an initiating maneuver, followed by a response and some reaction. The last two moves fall into the reflexive maneuver category. Defining the cycle and the maneuvers within the cycle permitted the researchers to look for recurring sequences in verbal behavior of the classroom and thus to view carefully the "ebb and flow" of the teaching process over greater lengths of time.

Besides the pedagogical moves, teaching cycles, and maneuvers found in teaching, Bellack sought to gather data in the second major area, meaning of the content of classroom discourse. Bellack defined four different kinds of meaning in the verbal behavior of students and teachers: (a) substantive with associated (b) substantive-logical meanings, (c) instructional with associated (d) instructional-logical meanings. Substantive means the subject matter and the specific concepts and generalizations to be taught. Substantive-logical refers to the cognitive processes involved in dealing with the subject matter, such as defining, interpreting, explaining, fact stating, opining, and justifying. Instructional involves such things as making assignments and routine classroom procedures that are part of the instructional process. Instructional-logical refers to distinctively didactic verbal processes such as those involved in positive and negative evaluation, explaining procedures, and giving directions.[6]

In the final major area of interest in this research, that of emotional meaning, Bellack states:

Since it seemed reasonable to assume that our reactions to the emotional meanings expressed by teachers would be quite different from those of the typical high school students who participated in the research, it was decided that emotional meanings should be analyzed from the point of view of student observers.

The semantic differential technique was used to describe each teacher's emotional style in terms of the meanings he conveyed along three dimensions: valence, activity, and strength. Valence was described by the following scales: fair-unfair, positive-negative, and good-bad. Strength was described by hard-

[5] Bellack, *et al.* (2), pp. 6-7.

[6] Bellack, *et al.* (2).

soft, heavy-light, and strong-weak. Activity was described by alive-dead, hot-cold, and fast-slow.

Judges in this part of the study were 11th grade students in a communications class in a senior high school similar to those who participated in the experimental classes. Because of the confidential nature of the tape recordings, ratings were obtained only for thirteen teachers who consented to have recordings of their classes played for persons other than regular members of the research staff. These ratings served as the basis for analyzing the emotional meanings communicated by the teachers.[7]

A summary of the category system used by Bellack may be represented graphically as follows:

Pedagogical Moves

1. Structuring
2. Soliciting
3. Responding
4. Reacting

Teaching Cycles

1. Initiatory Maneuvers–Structuring and/or soliciting.
2. Reflexive Maneuvers–Responding and/or reacting.

Content Meanings[8]

1. Substantive Meanings
   - 1.1 Trade
     - 1.11 Trade–Domestic and International
     - 1.12 Trade–Money and Banking
     - 1.13 Trade–Who Trades with Whom
   - 1.2 Factors of Production and/or Specialization
     - 1.21 Factor of Production–Natural Resources
     - 1.22 Factor of Production–Human Skills
     - 1.23 Factor of Production–Capital Equipment
     - 1.24 Factors other than Natural Resources, Human Skills, and Capital Equipment Occurring in Discussions of Reasons for Trade.
   - 1.3 Imports and/or Exports
   - 1.4 Foreign Investment–General
     - 1.41 Foreign Investment–Direct
     - 1.42 Foreign Investment–Portfolio
   - 1.5 Barriers to Trade
     - 1.51 Barrier–Tariffs
     - 1.52 Barrier–Quotas
     - 1.53 Barrier–Exchange Control
     - 1.54 Barrier–Export Control
     - 1.55 Barrier–Administrative Protectionism
2. Substantive-Logical Meanings
   - 2.1 Analytic Process (analytic statements are statements about the proposed use of language and are true by virtue of the meaning of the words of which they are composed.)

[7] Bellack, *et al.* (4), p. 4.

[8] All content in this research came from a unit on "International Trade" based on the first four chapters of the pamphlet *International Economic Problems* by James D. Calderwood (Minneapolis: Curriculum Resources, 1961).

- 2.11 Defining–General (to give the defining characteristics of a class and to give a specific example of an item within a class.)
  - 2.111 Defining–Denotative (to refer to the objects to which a term is applicable.)
  - 2.112 Defining–Connotative (to give the set of properties or characteristics that an object must have for the term to be applicable.)
- 2.12 Interpreting (to give a verbal equivalent, usually for the purpose of rendering its meaning clear.)

2.2 Empirical Process (empirical statements give information about the world, based on one's experience of it.)

- 2.21 Fact Stating (to give an account, description, or report of an event or state of affairs.)
- 2.22 Explaining (to relate an object, event, action or state of affairs; to show the relation between an event or state of affairs and a principle or generalization; or to state relationships between principles or generalizations.)

2.3 Evaluative Process (evaluative statements are statements that grade, praise, blame, commend or criticize something.)

- 2.31 Opining (to make statements giving own valuation regarding (a) what should or ought to be done, or (b) fairness, worth, importance, quality of an action, event, person, idea, plan, or policy.)
- 2.32 Justifying (to give reasons for holding an opinion regarding (a) what should or ought to be done, or (b) fairness, worth, importance, quality of an action, event, policy, idea, plan, or thing.)

2.4 Not clear (when wording or sense of a statement is ambiguous and the substantive-logical meaning cannot be determined.)

3. Instructional Meanings

- 3.1 Assignment (discussion of reports, homework, debates, tests, readings, and the like.)
- 3.2 Material (discussion of textbooks, maps, chalkboard, teaching aids, films, newspapers, television programs, radio, and the like.)
- 3.3 Person (discussion of teacher's or pupil's person, physiognomy, dress, expression, or appearance.)
- 3.4 Procedure (discussion of any course of action or set of activities, continuing activity, or future activity.)
- 3.5 Statement (reference to any verbal utterance, particularly the meaning, validity, truth, or propriety of that utterance.)
- 3.6 Logical Process (discussion of the way language is used or of a logical process.)
- 3.7 Action–General (reference to performance, action, or event where the nature of the performance cannot be determined or when more than one of the sub-categories listed below are involved.)
  - 3.71 Action–Vocal (reference to action involving the emission of speech or sound.)
  - 3.72 Action–Physical (reference to action where physical movements are primary.)
  - 3.73 Action–Cognitive (reference to action where cognitive process is principally involved.)
  - 3.74 Action–Emotional (reference to action where feelings or emotions are principally involved.)

4. Instructional-Logical Meanings
    4.1 Analytic Process (same as substantive-logical meanings.)
        4.11 Defining—General
            4.111 Defining—Denotative
            4.112 Defining—Connotative
        4.12 Interpreting
    4.2 Empirical Process (same as substantive-logical meanings.)
        4.21 Fact Stating
        4.22 Explaining
    4.3 Evaluative Process (same as substantive-logical meanings.)
        4.31 Opining
        4.32 Justifying
        4.33 Rating (includes judgments about the truth or falsity, or appropriateness of preceding statements.)
            4.331 Positive (affirmative evaluation usually in a reaction to a statement.)
            4.332 Admitting (mildly accepting or equivocally positive evaluation usually in a reaction to a statement.)
            4.333 Repeating (implicit evaluation in reaction in which there is only a repetition, rephrasing, or restatement of a preceding move with no explicit evaluative comment.)
            4.334 Qualifying (indication of reservation, however mild or oblique usually in reactions to statements.)
            4.335 Not admitting (evaluations which reject by stating the contrary rather than by making an explicitly negative statement.)
            4.336 Negative (distinct evaluating usually in a reaction to a statement.)
            4.337 Positive or Negative (solicitations in which a request is made either for a positive or a negative evaluation.)
            4.338 Admitting or Not Admitting (solicitations in which a request is made to give an evaluation or to permit a given procedure or action.)
    4.4 Extralogical Process (solicitations which call for the performance of a physical or cognitive act or solicitations which invite responses that are nonpropositional verbal utterances; for example, commands, questions, or directives.)
        4.41 Performing (solicitations which ask or demand of someone to do something.)
        4.42 Directing (solicitations which ask for a directive or a further solicitation and must be general or involve more than one alternative.)

Emotional Aspects—(Semantic Differential Technique for Describing Teacher's Emotional Style)

1. Valence
    fair-unfair
    positive-negative
    good-bad
2. Potency
    hard-soft
    heavy-light
    strong-weak

3. Activity
   - alive-dead
   - hot-cold
   - fast-slow[9]

Within the context of this extensive investigation into the linguistic behavior of classroom participants, Bellack sought to determine also the attitude change and content learning that took place. Since attitude change and knowledge acquisition were important, both pre- and post-tests[10] were given in both areas to determine significant change. In subsequent research, the investigators would like to ascertain what kinds of classroom events are related to what kinds of learning outcomes. This would be different from looking at the relationships between discourse variables and measures of learning based on some notion of what should be learned. In other words, the research would look at descriptive outcomes (learning) to see what classroom events (teaching) made them possible.

The only control on this experimental project was content. This gave some limits for the research and provided a basis for determining changes in knowledge and for analyzing the substantive meanings of the classroom discussion. As mentioned above, this was accomplished by having all of the teachers teaching the same basic unit on "International Trade." The teachers were free to teach as they felt they should.

The fifteen classrooms were then taped on four consecutive sessions and the verbal discourse transcribed for analysis.

Upon the analysis of the data, some interesting findings were derived. Only some of the more salient aspects of the research findings will be presented at this time.[11] It should be noted that, at this stage of the total investigation by Bellack, the primary purpose was methodological in nature, to develop a system that would enable the researchers to describe reliably what was observed in terms of the conceptual system described above.

One of the interesting conclusions from this study was the fact that there were remarkable similarities among the teachers and classrooms in terms of pedagogical discourse. There was even a consistent and stable pattern in individual classrooms over the four sessions, regardless of the position in the unit of study. This was noted even when marked differences were observed in the teachers' experience and preparation and in the students' entire backgrounds. There appeared to be a basic pedagogical pattern of discourse with each participant playing specific roles in the classroom language game.

As might be expected, teachers were more active than students and

---

[9] Bellack, *et al.* (2).

[10] For a description of the testing measures see Bellack, *et al.* (2).

[11] For complete results and discussion on coding, testing, and other important measures of this research, see Bellack, *et al.* (2). Also, both reports are available in one volume: Bellack, Arno A. and others. *The Language of the Classroom.* New York: Teachers College Press, 1967. 274 pp.

tended to dominate the classroom verbal activity. Teachers spoke in a 3:1 ratio more frequently than the students, and initiated more pedagogical moves in a ratio of 3:2. Teachers also initiated about eighty-five percent of the teaching cycles (i.e. solicitation, response, and reaction), with the students initiating only fifteen percent.

The pedagogical roles that are played in the classroom, or the respective responsibility of the players, was easily discernable. The frequency of behavior in each category of pedagogical moves indicated that teachers are basically responsible for structuring and soliciting and mostly for reacting. Students play the role of respondents. The teachers, then, dominate three moves and the students one. Occasionally a pupil reacts, but rarely does he use the reacting move to rate previous action. In contrast the teachers most frequently used the reacting move to rate positively (i.e., "That's good!" or "That's not exactly right."). Students rarely used reacting to rate, and when they did it was mostly to rate fellow students.

About sixty percent of the moves in the classroom involved substantive meanings or the actual content of the lessons. Forty percent of the moves involved instructional meanings, and a large amount in this major category was involved with ratings. The substantive meaning categories varied most widely in the meanings expressed. Some teachers spent a great deal of time on "Barriers to Trade," some spent considerable time on "Free Trade," and some on "Imports—Exports," etc., thus reflecting the wide variety of time that was given to the substantive material under discussion. This great variability was most unusual to note, because the content (International Trade) was the only restriction placed on teachers, whereas in the pedagogical moves or the methodology there was great similarity. The teachers structured, solicited, and reacted in about the same proportion.

In terms of the logical processes in the classroom, sixty percent of the discussion was given to empirical processes (describing and explaining), less to the evaluative mode of giving opinions and justifying opinions and the analytic mode. Little time was spent discussing policy matters, what should or shouldn't be done in regard to international trade.

The pattern of communication in the classroom was mostly teacher-to-students and students-to-teacher. Very little pupil-to-pupil talk was recorded. The typical pattern was a teacher solicitation and a pupil response. This data reveals, of course, the importance of the question in the classroom.

This research also revealed some pertinent data on reactions. Since the typical teaching cycle was teacher solicitation, pupil responses, and teacher reaction, it was found that teachers react to seventy-five percent of all student responses, while pupils react to fellow students at only a three percent rate. This further substantiates the notion of rules being present in the classroom discourse game. Rules dictate that students do not react often. Eighty percent of the teachers' reactions to student responses involved ratings either positive or negative. All teachers were found to be much more positive than negative (4-1) in their ratings. They were just as positive to incongruent responses as to congruent responses in terms of expectations for a response. This is interesting and unexplainable at this time. Although pupils did not react often, when they did they reacted three times more frequently to teachers than to responses, which means that pupils enter into discussions when teachers invite them by solicitation. Students apparently do not feel free to come into a conversation again until the teacher reacts, and then they react to the teacher's reactions. Finally, teacher reactions that occasioned pupil reactions came mostly when substantive material was being discussed rather than a rating reaction by the teacher. In this case, then, if the teacher wants a reaction by students he might react by offering substantive material into the discourse rather than a rating.

Implications for Improved Teacher Education

Although he and his associates were concerned primarily with research rather than prescription of practice, there are a variety of implications arising from Bellack's work because of the basic descriptive nature of the investigation. First of all, his system of analysis is highly developed and can therefore be used as an analytic tool by preservice students to ascertain the kinds of linguistic behavior occurring in a regular classroom or in some simulated or laboratory teaching. The use of this tool for analyzing behavior brings to the level of awareness what is transpiring in a teaching situation and should cause more analytic behavior to result. Bellack feels that this system can be used in areas of the curriculum other than the specific area of International Trade and would require only a modification of his Substantive Meaning categories. The pedagogical moves, teaching cycles, and other content meanings would remain the same and should provide an adequate framework for analysis.

From a review of this system and some analysis of classroom discourse, the students can begin to develop an understanding of the different modes in teaching. They can ascertain and understand when a fact is being stated or defined, when a judgment is being made, and when justification or rating is occurring. Further, they can understand the basic pedagogical moves defined by Bellack in this study and view carefully the teaching cycles that occur in classroom linguistic behavior. From these basic understandings of moves, cycles, and modes, the teacher education instructor and his students can begin to make some assumptions, develop some limited models on teaching selected content, and then test and evaluate outcomes. The fact that Bellack's categories carefully describe the triangular relationships among teacher, student, and content lends itself well to some empirical and analytic testing of ideas. The development of theoretical frameworks for testing is considered important by Bellack for teacher education students, because this is where the awareness and analytic behavior on teaching starts.

Within the context of empirical development and testing of models derived from Bellack's work, the instructor and students might look specifically at some of the results of the study with the notion in mind that some change should occur in the existing pedagogical pattern now found in classrooms. This, too, would require some assumptions and informal testing. For example, the results of Bellack's study indicated that eighty-five percent of the questions in the classroom are asked by the teachers. Now, if it is felt that students should ask more questions and become better inquirers, then some thinking and investigation into different moves are required. The undergraduate education class could address its attention to this concern and develop different patterns for trial and evalution.

Another example could come from the distinct pattern in which communication is present in the classroom. Bellack found that the usual pattern was from teacher to student, then back to the teacher. If this is judged to be inadequate, the education class could search for different moves to change this pattern.

A final example would be a look at the question itself, because Bellack found the question to be a most important tool in the teaching process. A class might examine the kinds of questions asked, the pacing of the questions, and the kinds of responses that are required. Some developmental work and testing could be done in this area so that more desirable outcomes would result. Bellack suggests that this activity may have to be performed on an informal basis, because there is little evidence on questioning presently available. However, this activity lends itself well to analytic testing in laboratory situations.

Some other areas that might be judged significant for investigation could be teacher domination of classroom verbal activity, teacher and student reactions to responses, and the fact that sixty percent of the classroom discussion dealt with fact stating and explaining. These and many other results obtained from Bellack's extensive study could be investigated with development and testing following. The requirements for such an effort are a study of Bellack's investigation, an understanding of the various categories, the making of some assumptions, and most of all some creative effort on the part of the education instructor and his students. If the outcome from the effort is more analytical behavior and better functioning of the teaching process, then perhaps this could be judged as a valid activity at the preservice level.

Bibliography

1. Bellack, Arno A., editor. *Theory and Research in Teaching.* New York: Bureau of Publications, Teachers College, Columbia University, 1963.

2. ———, and Davitz, Joel R. in collaboration with Kliebard, Herbert M. and Hyman, Ronald T. *The Language of the Classroom.* U. S. Department of Health, Education, and Welfare. Cooperative Research Program, Project No. 1497. New York: Institute of Psychological Research, Teachers College, Columbia University, 1963.

3. ———, in collaboration with Hyman, Ronald T., Kliebard, Herbert M. and Smith,

Frank L., Jr. *The Language of the Classroom,* Part II. U. S. Department of Health, Education, and Welfare. Cooperative Research Program, Project No. 2023. New York: Institute of Psychological Research, Teachers College, Columbia University, 1965.

4. ———, and Davitz, Joel R. in collaboration with Kliebard, Herbert M. and Hyman, Ronald T. *The Language of the Classroom.* U. S. Department of Health, Education, and Welfare. Cooperative Research Program, Project No. 1497. New York: Institute of Psychological Research, Teachers College, Columbia University, 1966. (A summary.)

5. ———, and Huebner, Dwayne. "Teaching." *Review of Educational Research* 30: 246-257; June 1960.

6. Kliebard, Herbert M. "The Observation of Classroom Behavior—Some Recent Research." *The Way Teaching Is.* Washington, D.C.: Association for Supervision and Curriculum Development, a department of the National Education Association, 1966.

Chapter 7. The Classroom Group and the School as a Unique Social System

Professor J. W. Getzels[1] and associate have developed a rather extensive system for the analysis of the school and classroom group as a unique social system and its meaning for goal behavior. In making this conceptual scheme of the social system explicit, they have identified the characteristics common to groups, and in particular to the classroom group, and have described in a conceptual framework the relationships of the characteristics in various dimensions for systematic analysis and study. This chapter will review the characteristics of a social system, its meaning for the classroom and school, and the explicit model for analysis, as well as the meaning of the work for the preservice teacher education process.

For the description of the characteristics of a classroom group, as in any group, Getzels has identified (a) goals, (b) participants, (c) leadership, and (d) relationships to other groups or institutions as the major items.[2] The major goal of the classroom and school is learning. This is, of course, the primary reason that the group gets together, and the school curriculum specifies these outcomes and procedures. The goal of learning as defined by content and method in the curriculum is stated before the group comes into being. This limits the definition of goals, at least of major goals, by the participating group.

The group participants in the school and class are generally defined, too. Mandatory participation by students is ruled by laws. Furthermore, the composition of the group is given before the group comes into being. Time of birth and place of residence dictate the class of participants more than choice or careful planning, and thus tend to define a group in a more or less random manner. The nature of group composition will, of course,

---

[1] Dr. Getzels is Professor of Education and Psychology at the University of Chicago.

[2] Getzels and Thelen (5).

have some effects on the learning that takes place and the social interaction present.

The control or leadership function falls into the hands of the teacher. Law and custom again prevail in this characteristic when the the professionally trained and legally certified person enters the group situation. The teacher in formal aspects holds a position that perhaps is contrary to the democratic process. He forms the ruling class in the group and is placed there without the consent of, or selection by, the group. Even though freedom can and does exist for group members, it has to be delegated by the leaders. In a legal sense group members, then, have really no control over their leadership.

Besides the three characteristics mentioned above, some consideration must be given to the relationship of the other groups and institutions. In the case of the classroom there are several relationships that exist. First of all, one class fits into a sequence of learning experiences and thus has a direct relationship to the preceding and succeeding classes. Membership in more than one school group by a participant is likely (i.e., membership in both an English and a gym class), so interrelationships exist here. Then the many organizations outside the school to which a classroom group participant may belong can cause many different relationship to exist. The student probably belongs to a family; some sort of gang or clique; a church; and some clubs and other organizations, both formal and informal, which may have more effect on his behavior than the actual classroom or school. Pressures and influence from these outside sources may effect a behavior which is incongruent with the desirable behavior of the classroom. Thus, a variety of factors play upon the behavior of the student when he is a participating member of the classroom group.

Besides the variety of pressures exerted on the class, the same outside pressures exist on the teacher and his behavior. Personal habits, political and religious affiliations, places of residence, and other characteristics of the teacher may be under careful scrutiny by parents and community. Besides the private aspects of a teacher's life, the professional life reflects pressures from a variety of directions. Many community members and parents exert pressures on the teacher that would not be exerted on other professional members of the community.

The causes of and concerns for the pressures exerted on the school and its classrooms in a way reflect a uniqueness that few, if any, other social systems must cope with while attempting to function properly. Each institution needs and perhaps demands certain things from the school to propagate existing conditions or to lead into what should emerge in society. This, then, is another unique characteristic of the classroom group: "There is nothing that goes on in the classroom that is not of ultimate consequence for the social order; and there is not much that is of immediate consequence for the social order that is not reflected in some way in the classroom."[3] From the above brief discussion of the characteristics of the school and

[3] Getzels and Thelen (5), pp. 60-61.

classroom group, it can be seen that a variety of factors, perhaps both good and bad, come into play when viewing this group as a social system. However, it is interesting to note that education generally is subscribed to strongly by most members of our democratic society.

From the above description of characteristics in the classroom, some interesting and pertinent issues can be raised which require a systematic analysis. Getzels says:

> 1. Learning in the classroom involves bringing about change through consciously planned experiences. This involves the exercise of conscious choice of alternatives. Question: How can we conceptualize the choices available to the teacher and the class?
>
> 2. The goals of learning, the procedures by which the goals will be achieved, and the subject-content to be learned are all more or less specified in advance, that is, they are "givens" in the classroom situation. Question: What are the sources of these givens, and what is the relative stability or modifiability of each?
>
> 3. The classroom is an "accidental" collection of persons, having little or no legitimate recourse from participating in a priori goals and procedures of the school. Question: What are the dimensions of the problem generated by this "accidental" and "enforced" nature of the classroom group, and what is the effect of these factors on classroom learning?
>
> 4. In addition to the problem of relating one's self to the associations and activities required in the classroom, each individual must also "gear in" his own needs, goals, and attitudes to the way of life that is prescribed in the classroom. Question: What is the relationship of this problem to the preceding one, and again what are the implications of this issue for classroom learning?
>
> 5. The teacher is in almost absolute authority in the sense that the only power students may legitimately have over the classroom group is that permitted or delegated by the teacher. Question: With respect to what kind of matters can the teacher delegate authority to students, and how may this transfer of power be accomplished?
>
> 6. The "accidental" and compulsory interaction in the classroom may be modified by students who set and enforce their own goals and standards within the classroom. Question: How does this occur, and what are the factors tending to encourage or discourage such development?
>
> 7. Every participant in the classroom group is also a member of numerous groups outside the classroom. Each is subject to various group pressures and loyalties which may be in opposition to each other. Question: What is the nature of the conflicts to which these pressures give rise, what are the differential reactions thereto, and what is the effect of such conflicts on classroom learning?
>
> 8. The classroom is part of the school, and the school is a central institution in the community. There is widespread public interest, pressure, and conflict with respect to the school as representative of the community. Question: What is the nature of these community pressures and conflicts, and how do they affect the classroom group?
>
> 9. The school as a central social institution is integrally related to the other institutions of the community. It may be an instrument for promoting change or of maintaining the status quo of these institutions and, accordingly, of the social order as a whole. Question: Under what circumstances does the

classroom serve in one capacity or the other, and what would be involved in changing the role of the school with respect to the other institutions?

10. Although the teacher is in many ways "trapped" by community pressures on his personal and professional status, there is, on the other hand, the powerful principle of "academic freedom" which protects the teacher's right to make choices for educational purposes. Question: What is the relationship between the type of choice the teacher makes and the kind of classroom learning situation that ensues?[4]

To provide some systematic meaning to the description of observed events, Getzels has moved to a conceptual analysis. In doing this, an explicit framework or model has been developed which can explain, relate, and clarify the variables that are important for the analysis of the classroom group and school as a social system and for the meaning of behavioral outcomes of participants.

The beginning of the conceptual scheme is the social system, which in this case can be either the classroom group or the school. This is to distinguish it from either all of society or an entire state. Within the system Getzels suggests that institutions are present which have both certain roles and expectations that are necessary for the fulfillment of the goals of the social system. Also, since the system contains individuals who possess distinct personalities and need-dispositions, the obvious interaction of the individuals comprises the group behavior. So it is possible to identify institutions as having certain roles and expectations, and individuals as having certain personalities and needs. The first set of factors is identified by Getzels as the sociological level or nomothetic (normative) dimension of activity in a social system; the second set is identified and termed the psychological level or idiographic (personal) dimension of activity in a social system.

The first dimension may be represented as follows:

Social system → Institutions → Roles → Expectations → Institutional Goal-behavior

This is to say then that a social system has institutions to carry on its functions. Within the institution certain people have roles to play to carry on the functions of the institution. Roles are what people are expected to do. Role expectations, then, define what should or should not be done and should, therefore, lead to the goal behavior of the institution.

The school and individual classroom can be defined as a social system, because they fit the schematic dimension described above. Goal behavior in schools or classes can be achieved by the integration of institutions, the definition of roles, and the setting of the expectations. One can quite accurately analyze the remaining factors in this sociological level when given only one factor. In other words, if the expectations were known, it could be predicted what role should be played in what institutions and what the goal behavior would be. This would be true only at the theoretical level where the roles were occupied by "constant" individuals.

However, since individuals are different and possess different per-

[4] Getzels and Thelen (5), pp. 63-64.

sonality traits, the psychological level comes into effect. Regardless of how structured the role will be and how clearly stated the expectations are, individuals will bring to the group idiosyncrasies which are theirs alone. Therefore, to determine specific behavior one must look at personality and individual need factors when considering group behavior. The individual dimension can be analyzed in a fashion parallel to that of the normative dimension. Instead of the institution we find, of course, the individual, who in turn possesses a personality defined by Getzels as "the dynamic organization within the individual of those need-dispositions that govern his unique reactions to the environment and to the expectations of the environment."[5] The analytic elements of the personality are, thus, the need-dispositions which lead in turn to the individual goal behavior. This individual dimension may be represented thusly:

Social system ➤ Individuals ➤ Personalities ➤ Need-dispositions ➤ Individual Goal-behavior

To bring together the knowledge of the specific behavioral aspects of the individual and the role expectation of the institution would provide a means of understanding the behavior and interaction of specific incumbents in a given institution.

Getzels combines the two dimensions and diagrammatically represents them as follows:

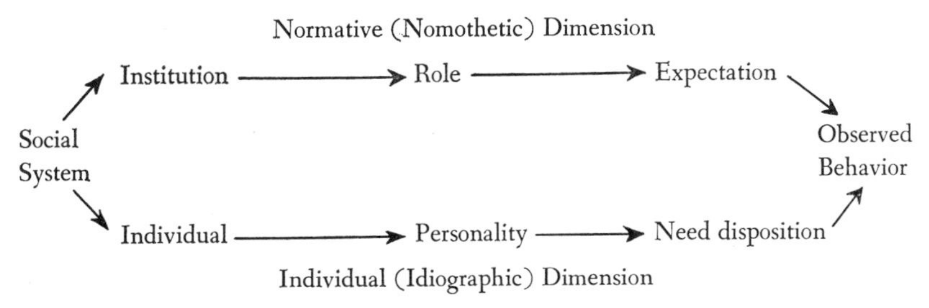

In the above diagram it can be seen that at the sociological level each social system has institutions to carry on its functions, with each institution being defined by the constituent roles. Each role is defined by the expectations of the role. At the psychological level the same reasoning holds true, with each unit serving as an analytic for the preceding one.

At this point one may view the social behavior of an individual by looking at the role-expectations and the personality-dispositions. As an individual reacts to a social system, he attempts to cope with the expectations within the framework of his individual personality. Thus, Getzels offers the formula of $B = f\ (RxP)$ where B is the observed behavior, R is the given institution role, and P is the personality of the role incumbent. In this case, the behavior of an individual is the function of the role and his personality. This formula for analysis takes on meaning for the educator in a variety of situations. Getzels cities the area of language arts, with the

[5] Getzels and Thelen (5), p. 68.

teaching of spelling and of creative writing as an excellent example. In the first case, spelling behavior will be more influenced by the role-expectation factor when a person adheres closely to the expectations of the school in becoming an effective speller. Personality is not involved nearly as strongly as the role expectations. In the case of creative writing, behavior should reflect more the personality-disposition level than the role, because it is an individual effort. Getzels states that these activities fall on a continuum, with role-relevant performance on one end and personality-relevant performance on the other. Thus, some classroom tasks require more adherence to one factor than the other, but of course, classroom behavior is a result of both factors, whose degree of importance depends on the task. Behavior, then, can be viewed as the line cutting between the role and the personality of the role incumbent. When the role expectation is maximized, personality still influences behavior, and vice-versa.

However, since the institution with its factors of role and expectations and the individual with his factors of personality and need-dispositions do not operate in a vacuum, Getzels moves on to look at the anthropological level of factors which play upon both the institution and the individual. The notions of culture, ethos, and values of both the institution and the individual enter into the picture when analyzing a social system and goal behavior.

The school as an institution finds itself embedded in a culture which possesses certain beliefs and characteristics (ethos), and these beliefs lead in turn to a value system held by the culture. These factors play upon the school with its role and expectations in the institution. This stratum, called anthropological by Getzels, adds another dimension to the model at the sociological or nomothetic level. This level can be viewed diagrammatically as follows:

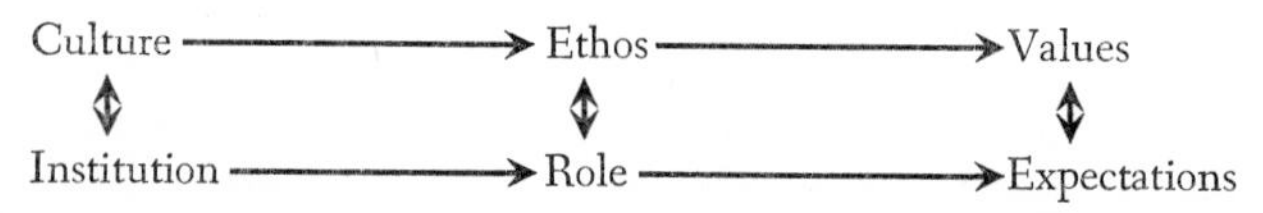

The reciprocal influence is indicated by the reversible arrows. At the anthropological level the values indicate what one ought to do, and this is reflected in the nomothetic level in expectations from the school.

Now Getzels builds the same case for the psychological dimension by stating that an individual is also related to the culture in which he has been reared. If an examination of the personality of an individual is important, one must go to the ethos in which he was raised. From there one is required to go to the values of individual culture, because in many ways the dispositions that individuals possess are derived from the values of the family, the neighborhood, and the social system in which the individual was brought up. This is the definition of socialization: the process of the individual's internalizing the values around him into his personal structure. Therefore, this anthropological level is necessary for analysis of goal behavior of the individual. The new stratum fits into the psychological dimension as follows:

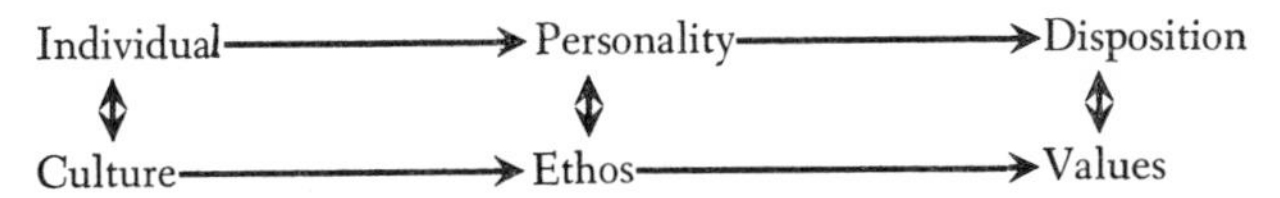

Again, the argument by Getzels states that the individual is embedded in a culture, and his personality and need-dispositions are affected by the culture's ethos and value system.

Putting the two major dimensions together reveals the following diagram:

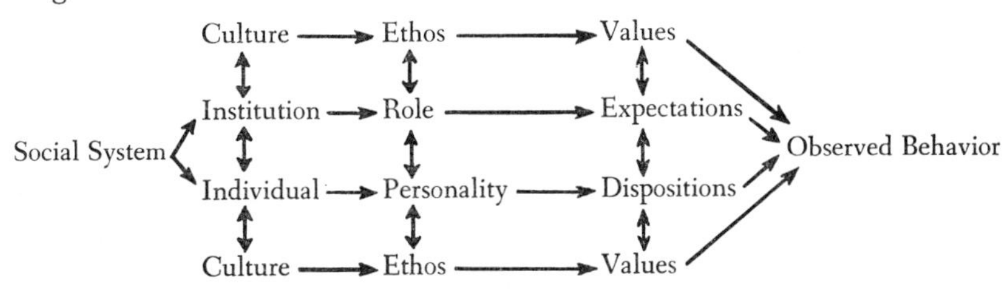

However, since there may be conflicts and deviant perceptions between the individual with his personality and need-dispositions and the institution with its role expectations, the group is defined and utilized to serve as a buffer. In this case the group mediates the institutional requirements and the individual dispositions. The group, then, deals with the conflicts in roles and the deviant perceptions of what should be, by supporting the institution in imposing certain normative role expectations on the individual, and also by supporting the individual in expressing certain idiosyncratic personality-dispositions.[6] The group, then, tends to impose a balance between the institution and the individual. To do this, the group develops a climate, which in turn can be analyzed into the constituent intensions of the group. The group climate represents the final dimension in the model. It is particularly important in the social system of the school. The stability and flexibility of the group depends on the degree of belongingness that the individual possesses as a group member. The greater the belongingness, the greater the communication between pupil and teacher, and the better the level of security for students. This would lead to a greater pride in the achievement of both institutional and individual goals. The group climate dimension is, thus, necessary for the effective functioning of an individual in an institution.

The final dimension of the model would be diagrammatically represented as follows:

Social System ——→ Group ——→ Climate ——→ Intensions ——→ Group Behavior

Putting all dimensions together would result in the following model:

[6] Getzels and Thelen (5).

Model for Analysis of a Social System and Goal-Behavior

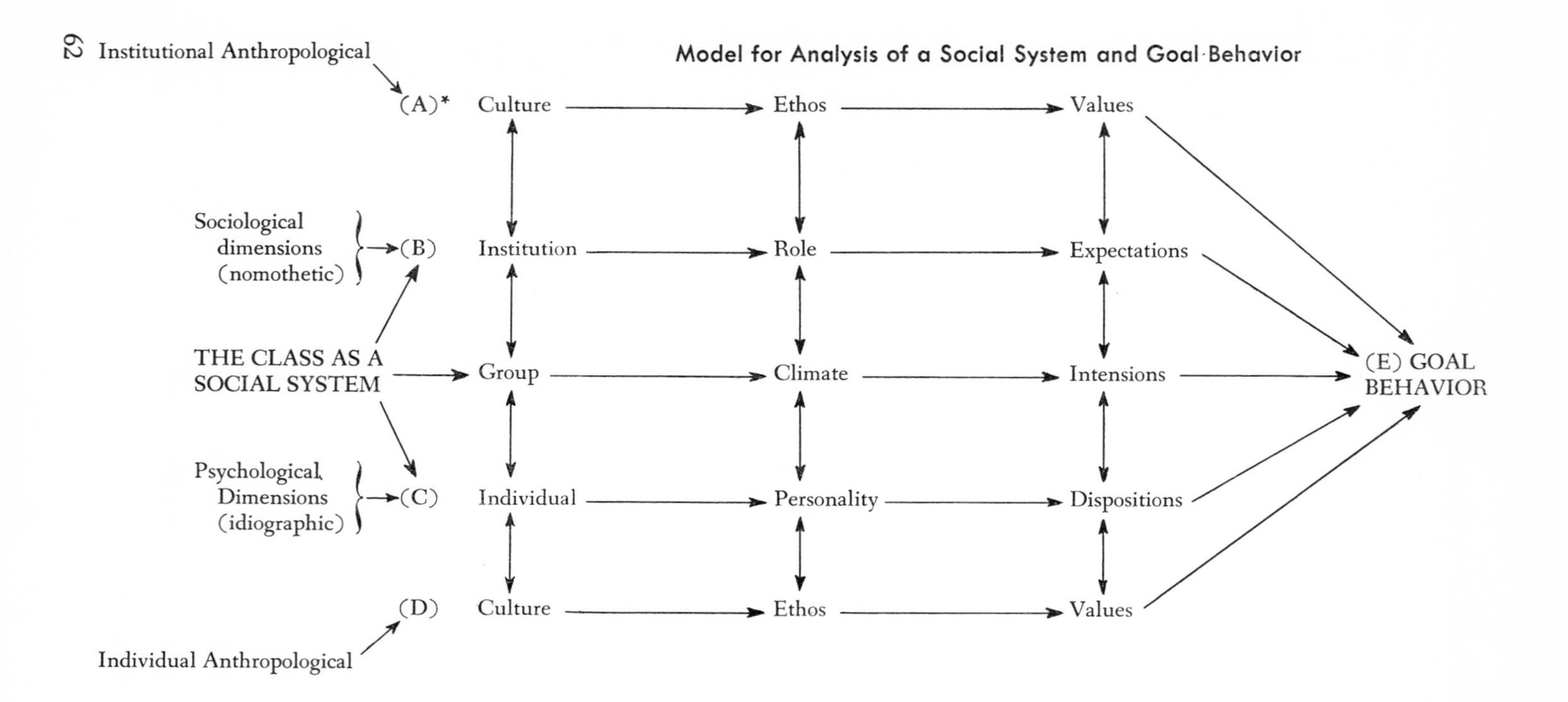

* Capital letters A through E will be discussed and used later in the chapter.

Once the model is developed, its applicability can be seen from a variety of uses. Getzels suggests that this model does not provide answers, but it is a tool to understand and describe behavior in a social system. Further, it helps to raise issues and questions to which the educator can address his attention.

Getzels cites an example of the use of this model and the problems and issues that are identified from a contemporary and currently popular notion in education, that of compensatory education for the culturally deprived.[7] If one were to ask the question, Can our schools presently serve the needs of the "culturally deprived"? this model might provide some interesting results for investigation. The complete model on page 62 has its institutional anthropological level identified with a capital letter A, the sociological level of institution-role-expectations as capital letter B, the psychological level as C, the individual anthropological level as D, and the goal behavior as E for purposes of this analysis.

Also, for purposes of this analysis, Getzels compares two social classes of children, the middle-class students and the lower-class students (those identified as "culturally deprived"), and the existing institution, the school.

It could be argued that the values which are related to the school by and large are the same values in which the middle-class child grows up. Most American schools are related to a set of values which are middle class in nature. Therefore, the values of the schools are congruent with the values of the stratum in which the child was reared, or $A \cong D$.

The role-expectation level of the school obviously tends to be similar to the cultural values at the anthropological level for reasons expressed before. In other words, the values of the culture are congruent with the expectations of the middle-class oriented school, or $A \cong B$.

The need-dispositions of the middle-class youngster are also obviously consistent with the cultural values in which he was reared, or $C \cong D$.

Then, since the above is true, from simple logic one can say that the need-dispositions of the middle-class child are congruent with the role expectations of the school ($C \cong B$), so the child generally comes set normally for school and its values, and goal behavior (E) can be achieved.

The middle-class youngster and his relationship to the school can be briefly stated by the following equations:

$A \cong D$ ($\cong$ means congruent)

$B \cong A$

$C \cong D$

$C \cong B$ and thus E is achieved

Now if the same kind of analysis is applied to the lower-class youngster ("culturally deprived") and the school, some different results occur.

For the lower-class youngster, the values set for the expectations in the normally middle-class school and the values which he has internalized

[7] Getzels, J. W. (6).

are not the same. For instance, the school expects the achievement ethic, but he does not see this and perhaps is lucky to see three meals a day. The lower-class culture has quite a different value system from that held by the school, so an incongruency exists, or $A \ncong D$.

Again, the role expectations of the predominantly middle-class school (B) and the cultural values of the community are congruent, as they were with the middle-class youngster, and curriculum expectations reflect the cultural values, or $B \cong A$.

Also, in the psychological dimension, the cultural values of the individual lower-class youngster are congruent with his personality-need-disposition. In the lower class, the youngster will generally reflect the values of the system in which he was reared, or $C \cong D$.

However, with simple logic again, it can be noted that the need-dispositions of the lower-class youngster brought to the school are incongruent with the role expectations of the school, or $C \ncong B$, and thus little goal behavior (E) is achieved.

The lower-class youngster and his relationship to the generally middle-class school can be briefly stated by the following equations:

$A \ncong D$

$B \cong A$

$C \cong D$

$C \ncong B$ and thus E is not achieved.

From using Getzels' model in this particular school-culture-individual concern, it can be seen that problems are identified. From the above analysis of the lower-class student, one might suggest a change in either D, the individual cultural level, or in B, the role-expectations of the school, to make the youngster more compatible with the school. Note here that the model only identifies problem areas, but does not suggest how the incongruities should be changed. This is an excellent example of the use and meaning of the Getzels model for analytic purposes in a major area involving the total model.

Getzels suggests that this model can serve to determine specific issues within the school itself. Issues such as the conflict between role-expectation and personality-disposition and role conflict itself can be identified by the use of the model.[8] One can simply analyze the factors, which in turn reveal the inconsistencies for corrective purposes.

Finally, Getzels suggests that the model can be used to understand problems that may be present between the school and outside value systems. In other words, the conflict between the cultural values outside the school and the institutional expectations within the classroom can be understood by applying the model. This application can help identify the issues that arise between "double standards" or "double value systems" between school and community, parents, children, etc.

---

[8] For discussion on conflict and analysis with the model, see: Getzels and Thelen (5).

Implications for Improved Teacher Education

Professor Getzels' model for the analysis of a social system has considerable meaning for education. First of all, it is a comprehensive attempt to bring together the variety of factors present in the school and the individual who attends the school. It also indicates clearly the relationship of the variables and how they play on one another. Because of its comprehensiveness, the model is applicable to any social system, be it a small group, class, school, or community. Finally, it brings the sociological factors of the school together with the psychological characteristics of the individual in the institutional setting of the school for the purposes of looking at the observed behavior resulting from such interaction.

Since the school is embedded in a culture and reflects cultural mores and values, and since the individual finds himself within a similar situation, the teacher must have a tool to analyze the factors in order to effect the desirable kinds of behavior compatible with individual needs and school and cultural expectations. This could be considered the major goal of the educative process, and Getzels' model can assist the teacher in analyzing the factors for effective teaching. This in itself makes the model a meaningful tool to be discussed and used at the preservice level.

The teacher education instructor and his students can begin to utilize the model once a purpose has been established. The purpose, of course, indicates what it is the model will do, or what should be found out regarding a social system. From a clear statement of purpose the instructor and students can begin to analyze the factors within the model. For a concluding example of the value of the model, one might look at cultural values and school expectations.

If one were to look at an upper-middle-class community and its relationship with and effects on school expectations, some interesting results might be revealed. The analysis of the expectations of the school, particularly for bright or gifted students, would suggest: (a) a work-success ethic, or having the children work up to ability; (b) a future-time orientation, or giving up the present for a bright and achieving future; (c) an emphasis on the creative and imaginative, with stress in the curriculum for individuality; and (d) a strong commitment to a set of values and special consideration for gifted children.

Then a visit to the community where the parents might display a different set of values, corresponding to the expectations of the school, could reveal: (a) no work-success ethic, but instead an ethic of sociability; (b) a present-time orientation, or "buy now and pay later" attitude; (c) little individuality, but mostly conformity to what others do; and (d) no real commitment to any set of values, but more of a moral relativism where if most people think something is right, it's right.[9]

It is obvious from an analysis of this sort that the values of the community and the expectations of the school truly contradict one another

[9] Getzels, J. W. (3).

by the "double standard" set. Stresses and strains on the youngsters could result from such incongruent conditions. Again, the model helps the educator to understand the conditions and resulting behavior, but does not provide any solutions.

The model, then, brings to the level of awareness the conditions that are present in a social system. This is all Getzels purports that it will do. But the fact that the model considers the sociological and psychological levels in the social system and the outcome of goal behavior would make it a valuable instrument for teacher education students to understand and utilize in their preparatory program.

Bibliography

1. Getzels, J. W. "A Psycho-Sociological Framework for the Study of Educational Administration." *Harvard Educational Review* 22: 235-246; 1952.
2. ———, and Guba, E. G. "Social Behavior and the Administrative Process." *Social Review* 65: 423-441; 1957.
3. ———. "The Acquisition of Values in School and Society." *The High School in a New Era.* Edited by F. S. Chase and H. A. Anderson. Chicago: University of Chicago Press, 1958, pp. 146-161.
4. ———. "Administration as a Social Process." *Administrative Theory in Education.* Edited by Andrew W. Halpin. Chicago: Midwest Administration Center, University of Chicago, 1958.
5. ———, and Thelen, Herbert A. "The Classroom Group as a Unique Social System." *56th Yearbook, the Dynamics of Instructional Groups: Part II.* Chicago: National Society for the Study of Education, 1960. Chapter 4, pp. 53-82.
6. ———. "A Social Psychology of Education." Edited by G. Lindzey and E. Aronson. *Handbook of Social Psychology.* Revised edition. Cambridge: Addison-Wesley Publishing Co. (in press).

Chapter 8. The Uses of Knowledge

Professor Harry Broudy[1] and his associates have done some extensive thinking regarding the identification and description of the uses of schooling, learnings, and knowledge, the terms of which are used interchangeably here. In this chapter the uses will be discussed, and the meaning that these distinct processes have for improved teacher education will be examined.

To begin with, Broudy suggests that throughout the ages the style of education, or better perhaps, the kind of learning, that was emphasized in schools has reflected the values or success routes held by the dominant groups in the contemporary society. The knowledge of current worth most always became the goal of the school. In the twenties the connection between society and school in the realm of knowledge was reflected in the curriculum offerings where emphasis was placed on skills and knowledge necessary to acquire and hold a certain job. Later on the curriculum reflected such values as family membership and emotional maturity. Currently the big emphasis is on the knowledge of science and technology.

This "knowledge of greatest worth" concept presents complications in curriculum building, especially when consideration is given to the necessary learnings for preparation of each individual young person in the school. If one were to analyze and list the variety of specific skills, attitudes, principles, and information necessary for an individual's preparation, and in turn for his success route, the variety would lead to a point where there would be little common education in the school. Virtually all young people would be going in different directions. It is within the context of common education, or more specifically general education, that Broudy addresses his attention to the uses of schooling. The terms "common" and "general," though related, are not synonymous. Common in this case refers to whatever the total population of the school studies, where general "refers or could refer to a characteristic of the subject being studied."[2] General, then, is the

[1] Dr. Broudy is Professor of Philosophy of Education at the University of Illinois.

[2] Broudy, Smith, and Burnett (1), p. 44.

opposite of specific and thus likely would be more abstract than concrete. It is within the major framework of a general education that Broudy and colleagues have identified the uses of schooling.

Broudy suggests that the school's role in a highly developed society is to equip the student with knowledge and the disposition to use it in behalf of three purposes:

1. to perform his civic duties, i.e., to discharge his obligation to family, clan, state, and country.
2. to produce and consume goods and services.
3. to cultivate his power for achieving the ideals of characters, i.e., of the ideal happiness.[3]

The first two goals are those of the social cluster in which people live out their days; the third is what is supposed to justify the first two. The first two goals are social and practical in that they enable people to do what it takes to keep the group strong and prosperous; the last goal is individual and represents the intellectual and practical excellences of the day as embodied in a personal style of life. It is interesting to note that the state, which manages the whole enterprise, forgives the citizen's failure to achieve happiness more readily than shortcomings in meeting his economic and civic obligations.

In the above context, the school reflects through its learnings and knowledge what is currently important for society. Today, the paradigm of learning is furnished by the way we use scientific concepts in technology. In every period, therefore, there is a danger that the schools will overstress one type of learning to the exclusion of others. This could be identified as a danger if there are different uses of knowledge and if all of the uses are valuable. Broudy suggests that this is happening today; thus the examination of uses is imperative for the adequate functioning of the school.

Four Uses of School Learnings

The four typical uses of school learnings are replicative, associative, applicative and interpretive. A discussion of these uses, starting with the associative, follows.

Associative Use of Knowledge

Learning is used associatively when something learned comes to mind because it has something in common with the present situation. When a student is requested to respond to a question, he resurrects from memory something or other that the question suggests. In this case, then, "the laws of association—resemblance, contiguity, and satisfaction—purport to tell what learnings the given cue is most likely to elicit."[4] The resemblance, contiguity, and satisfaction can determine what is associated with what.

[3] Broudy (5).

[4] Broudy, Smith, and Burnett (1), p. 46.

Some learnings become so much an intimate part of individuals that they fade out of direct awareness to a point where individuals do not think about them. They are perhaps forgotten, or are not explicitly at the level of consciousness. Then upon a cue or some association they are brought back to the conscious level. The associative use of learning is precisely the selective forgetting (or selective storage and retrieval) that makes the individual unique. Perhaps the individual forgets and remembers as his needs dictate. Broudy suggests that Latin may be an example of associative learning. The words "transport" and "transpire," to the individual who has previously studied Latin, have an image of "carry across" or "breathe across." To those not exposed to Latin, the response image might be "moving something from one place to another" for transport, or "something happening" in the case of transpire.[5] The image came from a previous learning in Latin, and even the fact that those who have studied it previously would not fare well on a current Latin test does not destroy the fact that the learnings still function at the subliminal level.

The associative use of knowledge can easily be confused with logical responses. An example of this case from Broudy, *et al.*, is, "If the teacher asks, 'why is the sun hot?' the pupil may reply, 'because it is round and bright.' This is not a logical answer, although it is understandable as an associative use of learning, because the sun is round and it is bright."[6] The argument goes on to suggest that students and teachers alike are not sufficiently sensitive to this important distinction. Many essay questions are answered by students responding with things recalled in some fashion or other by parts of or the entire question. Since the response is not false, and since it may have been written well, it may often be acceptable even if logically irrelevant. The teacher's cue in the question invoked a recall of associated ideas. The psychological response, relevant to the question but logically irrelevant, indicates the use of associative learnings and points again to the need for a careful understanding of this process. The teacher must know when he is involving the associative use of knowledge and when he is encouraging logical thinking.

Besides the understanding of the associative use of knowledge and its possible incongruity with logical thinking, Professor Broudy suggests other important features for an adequate understanding. Because it is most difficult to measure the associative use of learnings by tests, it is greatly undervaluated by school people. But what about the appreciation of the arts, such as poetry, fiction, and drama? The imagery involved in reading poetry, fiction, and drama depends a great deal on past learnings that may not be recalled exactly as learned. If one were to read, "This is the forest primeval/the murmuring pines and the hemlocks," an eerie feeling of great age and an aura of mystery about the murmuring pines and hemlocks might result. However, has anyone heard a tree murmur? Yet the individual might understand exactly and feel precisely what it means for a tree to

[5] Broudy (5).
[6] Broudy, Smith, and Burnett (1), p. 47.

murmur or sigh.[7] Now, one might ask when this act of learning occurred for the individual, and how can he recall it? This is the associative use of knowledge.

Because of the aesthetic value of the associative learning, it is well to understand the processes of such use. Since it is difficult to trace the origin of such school learnings, to determine what will be forgotten, or to determine what will be used, this is a most difficult use of knowledge to analyze. Since it does help in the appreciation of the arts and since it distinguishes much of what has gone on before, the teacher may (and perhaps should) be free to teach some things of this nature without a high degree of prediction for success.

Replicative Use of Knowledge

As distinguished from the associative use of knowledge which is so difficult to identify and describe, the replicative use is most definite; it reinstates the original learning on appropriate cue. Thus, if one is asked to sign an order or a receipt, he can repeat a set of motions that he has performed many times. The most notable example of this is in the practice of skills, and in rote memorization and recall of facts. The traditional emphasis on reading, writing, and arithmetic displays a heavy reliance upon the replicative use of knowledge in school. Broudy suggests that this use of learning has been at times, and perhaps at all times, synonymous with schooling. The overlearning of performance skills in the elementary school emphasizes the replicative use of school learning.

One might tend to play down this use of schooling because it is of a lower level than thinking and reasoning. But one must have selected facts, elements, and particulars with which to think, and these are learned as given. At the other end of the continuum, however, one might tend to place too much emphasis on this use of knowledge.

Professor Broudy argues that the spread of knowledge currently before us should imply teaching as few particulars as possible. The number of particulars learned for replication has to be kept to a minimum for fairly obvious reasons. Because of these major concerns, it would appear necessary to think carefully about this use of knowledge and its meaning for young people. The important concern here may be to teach this use of schooling as efficiently and painlessly as possible; this may be where programmed instruction can find its way into meaningful use in schools. Also, some thought on fact storage and the use of the computer may be necessary in this area. The statement and recall of facts and the extensive practice of skills are concerns that have faced educators since the beginning of schooling. One must be aware of what schooling can and cannot do for the student. Some facts and skills are important and indispensable to life and thought; but they will neither supply all of the responses life will call upon the students to make, nor will they in and of themselves generate the rules

---

[7] Broudy (5).

and principles that enable students to create answers to unpracticed questions. This leads to the need for the last two uses of learning.

Applicative Use of Learning

The very serious shortcoming of replicative use of knowledge is its inflexibility. It can be used only when a similar replicative situation arises. Thus, one must identify another use of knowledge that can apply to other situations. In this case, then, it is expected that curriculum time and school resources would be devoted to studies that could be applied, and that schooling would be evaluated in terms of its being applicable. This may be particularly true now, when science and technology are the critical factors in industry, health, war, and peace.

Applicative uses of knowledge are school learnings in the form of some principle, generalization, or statement of fact used to solve a problem or analyze a particular situation.[8] The applicative use of schooling, though it enhances the power of understanding and control, is not an easy task. Applying knowledge can occur when one recognizes an object or event as covered by a major generalization or law, or when one sees some resemblance of a problem-situation to another situation previously incurred. "This type of application may be thought of as filling in the missing terms of a proportional equation."

$$\frac{\text{Familiar Problem}}{\text{New Problem}} \qquad \frac{\text{Familiar Solution}}{?(\text{New Solution})}$$ [9]

One would simply fill in the three "givens" and complete the solution of the problem.

"As an example, we might consider the familiar situation of boys in slum neighborhoods resisting delinquency when an extensive recreational program is introduced. If another neighborhood is afflicted by a high rate of juvenile delinquency, it occurs to us to apply to a familiar solution; namely, instituting recreational facilities."[10] This does not, however, denote original application, because someone had to apply some knowledge to the original problem of delinquency rate and recreational activities. Also, to solve the same problem several times in the same way would remove this use of knowledge from the applicative and place it in the replicative realm.

Broudy suggests that the applicative use of academic knowledge is relatively rare in ordinary life, and that the scholar and researcher are the ones who really apply knowledge at its highest level. When the scholar applies knowledge it is, in fact, a way of expanding knowledge itself, rather than merely understanding it. Even though problem solving is taught in schools with hopes of a carry-over in life, life's problems are so complex that a skilled individual is required to work with them. We apply knowl-

---

[8] From Broudy, Smith, and Burnett (1).

[9] *Ibid.*, p. 51.

[10] *Ibid.*

edge in our specialities. One distinction Professor Broudy makes between applicative and interpretive uses of knowledge is that applicative use involves carrying out a process for problem solving, whereas interpretive use of knowledge (to be discussed next) is satisfied by understanding the process.

To apply knowledge one needs a device that translates knowledge into strategies and processes for action on particular situations, i.e., rules and procedures. This device could be considered a technology. Having applicative knowledge does not mean applying the process, but it does mean having planned or devised a carrying-out process. Just where to insist on overt action in the applicative use of knowledge is not clear. Obviously, a physicist who uses physics to think up a role of engineering practice, the engineer who designs the bridge, and the worker who builds the bridge may all be applying knowledge. Yet, it is clear that each is operating at a different level of concreteness. It might be said, then, that to apply knowledge *K* is to prescribe a set of rules and procedures for a domain of objects not directly or explicitly included in the domain of *K* yet which can be subsumed under the principles of *K*.[11]

The difference between interpretive and applicative use is supported by the fact that inventors are not always, or even generally, the same men who discover the knowledge to be applied.

There is also a difference between understanding a technology and using such knowledge applicatively. One can understand how a carburetor functions in an automobile but not know how to install one, repair one, or judge what is wrong with it. The familiarity with the appearance, construction, and norms of carburetors does not follow from (because it is not contained in) the knowledge of the principles of combustion or even in the principles of carburetor construction.

Interpretive Use of Knowledge

As seen immediately above, the interpretive use of knowledge is closely related to applicative use but is far less specific and detailed. This identified use of schooling could be defined as those learnings which are used to perceive, understand, or feel life situations; and it is a process primarily for orientation and perspective rather than action and problem solving.[12] The interpretive use of schooling, then, is the most fundamental of all, because without some interpretation of a situation it might not be possible to know whether to replicate, associate, or apply.

To understand something is, first of all, to identify it as belonging to a class or to a context that is already familiar. It can be said that a hurricane and a tornado are both to be understood as cousins in a family of violent storms. It is doubtful that even the most common perceptions—seeing or hearing this or that—are wholly devoid of these classifying and ordering

[11] Broudy (5).

[12] Broudy, Smith, and Burnett (1).

operations. This neither means that there is no common world to be perceived nor that every perception is a subjective law unto itself. It does mean that every time one is aware of anything he is aware also of what it is. If this is not the case, then puzzlement occurs and understanding does not take place. The interpretation of the impact of the world occurs through the use of meaning systems, categories, and structures. These are all names given to the frames of experience. Experience is ordered in frames of space, time, conservation of substance, reversibility of operations (Piaget), and the more developed systems of meaning called sciences and the humanities—the intellectual disciplines. They are disciplines because they are systems of controlled thinking and meaning. They are systematic ways of sorting experiences and provide designs for resorting them.

For example, if one were to understand the war in South Vietnam, it would mean, among other things, that a person can:

1. locate the scene of conflict on a map.
2. recount the series of major events that led up to the war.
3. name the alleged goals of the parties in the conflict.
4. talk about the troops and the battles.
5. talk about the diplomatic maneuvers.[13]

In summary, a rough but practical test for understanding is the kind of behavior called talking, discussing, and reading about the South Vietnamese situation. It should be noted, however, that understanding the war does not entail doing something about it. Action on *X* is not a necessary condition for understanding it. Knowledge is. A variety of learnings has gone into the task of understanding the event, and Broudy would suggest that this variety of learnings is like a set of maps to help people interpret and understand an event.

Even though the act of understanding is not totally clear, some of the learnings with which a person thinks or understands can be identified. Among them are the school subjects—all of them. The more general and extensive the schooling has been, the greater is the number of "maps" and conceptual schemata at a person's disposal. In short, one can understand *X* or interpret *X*: (a) when he can describe the system of meanings in which it is embedded; and (b) when he discerns the position of *X* in this system, i.e., when he can relate it to other elements of the system.

Finally, Broudy suggests that interpretation is not all intellectual, because all experience passes through a person who has definite values, tastes, and norms. These evaluative filters or maps color what he perceives. Cognitive interpretation and valuative interpretation go together; desires direct knowings and knowings shape desires but are not identical and cannot be treated as such. Generally, the sciences focus on the cognitive and the arts on the valuative.

Professor Broudy and his colleagues build a strong case for the inter-

[13] Broudy (5).

pretive use of schooling, which in turn means a general education for all young people at the secondary level. They feel that understanding—the goal of the interpretive use of schooling—is the basic development of cognitive maps on the phenomena which confront the young student and which is most important at this state of development. Therefore, general education, if it is successful, lays the necessary groundwork for all high-grade applicative uses of knowledge, because all uses of knowledge are in some sense interpretive, just as they are replicative and associative. The highly technical applicative use of academic knowledge as found in specialized education should occur when a person applies knowledge later on in life as he specializes in his chosen vocation. Therefore, understanding must come at the public school level before performance at the adult level. Technology—or the applicative use—thus requires the understanding or the interpretive use of knowledge to become truly effective.

Implications for Improved Teacher Education

The work of Professor Broudy on the four uses of schooling which correspond to the four uses of knowledge again provides a system for analysis and direction. This system affords a look at the uses of schooling and the meaning each has for the educative process.

It should be noted by now that the various uses are associated with the kinds of total outcomes desired by educators. The applicative use of schooling has direct meaning for the goal of vocational education and for problem-solving goals. As noted earlier, this use was held in high regard during the 1920's. The interpretive use of schooling is more appropriate for a general education, which is the major interest of Broudy and colleagues. Replicative use of school learnings finds its meaning in the skill development area.

After a study of the uses of knowledge by the teacher education instructor and his students, some notions about their meaning and significance can be developed. The preservice student must have an understanding of the uses, because what obviously will be taught corresponds to the uses. Therefore, an examination of the replicative use and what it can and cannot do, the associative, interpretive, and applicative, bring the student to the level of awareness for effective teaching and uses of schooling. The understanding of the uses should go beyond immediate outcomes and look at long-range goals. This activity, of course, requires some value judgments, which in turn can be made from a thorough study of the uses of schooling. The teacher must make the decision on what he wants as an outcome.

It would also appear important that a prospective teacher have a good knowledge of the content area to be taught, to enable him to make appropriate judgments and identify the important areas (concepts, principles, and generalizations) within the given content.

At this point, then, the prospective teacher can select some content and teach it in a simulated or regular situation for a specific goal. It should be noted again that one must teach directly for a use of schooling. The methodology of the classroom conforms to the uses of the knowledge desired. If one wants to teach an arithmetic lesson to insure understanding, he will use the interpretive use of knowledge to help his students interpret, understand, and perhaps generalize about some process or concept in arithmetic. Replicative use of schooling cannot achieve this goal, because no amount of drill can produce full understanding of the stated concept or process. Or if one wants to teach some applicative use of a scientific concept, then he must be concerned with the rules and procedures for application. Finally, if one wants to teach the skill of handwriting, he uses the replicative. It can be seen, therefore, that the uses of knowledge must be reflected in the methodology of the lesson. Incongruities in this approach will not produce the desired outcome.

This study and employment of the uses of schooling lend themselves well to an analytic or perhaps laboratory kind of preservice study. Students can analyze lessons and tests to determine the uses of knowledge involved, and they can select a use and determine the appropriate strategy or maneuver for some analytical teaching of their own. An assessment could be made, followed by some reteaching.

Regardless of where this study of the uses of schooling is conducted, be it in methods courses, in curriculum, or in a laboratory setting, it brings to the prospective teacher an awareness of the value and meaning of a most important area. Further, it can cause him to search for consistency in goal-statement and methodology. These would develop the kind of analytical teacher desirable for the classroom and for effecting the needed outcomes in public school work.

Bibliography

1. Broudy, Harry S., Smith, B. O., and Burnett, Joe R. *Democracy and Excellence in American Secondary Education.* Chicago: Rand McNally & Co., 1964.
2. ———. *Building a Philosophy of Education.* Englewood Cliffs, N. J.: Prentice-Hall, 1961.
3. ———. "Laboratory, Clinical, and Internship Experiences in the Professional Preparation of Teachers." *Ideas Educational* (The Kent State University School) 2: 5-14; Spring 1964.
4. ———. *The Scholars and the Public School.* (Bode Memorial Lecture) Columbus, Ohio: College of Education, The Ohio State University, 1963.
5. ———. "The Uses of Schooling." Paper delivered as part of lectures at the State University College, Geneseo, New York, February 10, 1966.

Chapter 9. Logical Structure of Teaching

Doctors Albert E. Hickey and John M. Newton[1] have conducted an intensive investigation into the logical order of teaching within the field of programmed learning, sponsored by the Office of Naval Research. Some very pertinent and selected aspects of this research will be discussed in this chapter, and the meaning that they hold for improved teacher education will conclude the discussion.

In this investigation, Hickey and Newton have given particular attention to the knowledge space. For adequate cognition and learning, a schema for the organization of things known or knowable is important. In the case of adequate cognition, Hickey has suggested that the problem of induction versus deduction always comes into effect. Often induction is defined as reasoning from specific to general, and deduction, the opposite. However, specific is confused with concrete or elemental, and general with abstract or complex; and this is particularly true when discussing induction and deduction in terms of concept formation strategies.

In pointing out the confusion, Hickey and Newton mention that there are at least three definitions of induction used in connection with programmed instruction. They are as follows:

1. A program is inductive if it begins by defining the most elementary units of a concept and progressively combines these into more complex units until the final concept is attained. This definition is one of overall direction, from elementary definitions or subconcepts to the final major concept or principle. An inductive program may also have deductive sub-routines.
2. A program is inductive if it progresses from concrete to abstract levels of description. For instance, a given law of economics may be presented on at least four levels of abstraction. The most concrete level would have the learner actually observe market transactions at the

[1] Dr. Hickey, a psychologist, is the President of ENTELEK, Incorporated, of Newburyport, Mass. Dr. Newton is Associate Professor of Psychology, University of Omaha.

neighborhood grocery store. Or the law may be presented at a somewhat less concrete level by simulating the activity in the grocery store with detailed verbal description. In the third instance, it will be less concrete and more abstract to describe the economic law in terms of market transactions in general. Finally, the least concrete and most abstract way to describe the law is with mathematical symbols.

3. Perhaps the most common definition of an inductive program is that it presents examples from which the learner must derive the concept or parts of the concept. This seems simple enough, but in the light of the two previous definitions it becomes more complex. For instance, what type of examples are used? Are they concrete or abstract? Do the examples begin by illustrating the final concept, or do they illustrate basic units of concept first?[2]

Since the real confusion about induction and deduction stems primarily from the terms specific, concrete, and elementary on the one hand, and abstract and general on the other, Hickey and Newton have addressed their attention to these areas in their research. Also, since analysis and synthesis and the structure of knowledge play important roles in learning and concept formation, some considerable attention has been given to them here. These researchers have developed significant models for use in these areas which have considerable meaning for the logical structure of teaching.

The first model was developed to indicate the relationship of the sub-concepts or conceptual elements to the major concepts. The Logic Tree which they devised (see Figure I) does this in the experimental content area of economics and the major concept of "Law of Demand." By proceeding from top to bottom, the conceptual elements are assembled in a broader, more complex concept, a process called synthesis. To move in the opposite direction, it can be noted that the complex concept is separated into its more elemental components; this process is called analysis.

Further, the model shows the relationship between general rules, principles, or laws and specific instances or examples of the principles. And it helps distinguish concrete, "point-at-able" events or phenomena from more abstract representations of those events and their interaction.[3]

In this model,

> The most primitive or elemental forms are at the top, and are successively combined to form relatively more complex terms or sub-concepts. The sequence in which the elemental terms are added to the "root" concept, increasing its complexity, can be graphically demonstrated by tracing the tree from "purchase" down to the next node where "purchase" is combined with the element "unit

---

[2] Hickey and Newton (2), pp. 3-4.

[3] Hickey and Newton (2).

Figure I.—Logic Tree for concept: Law of Demand.[4]

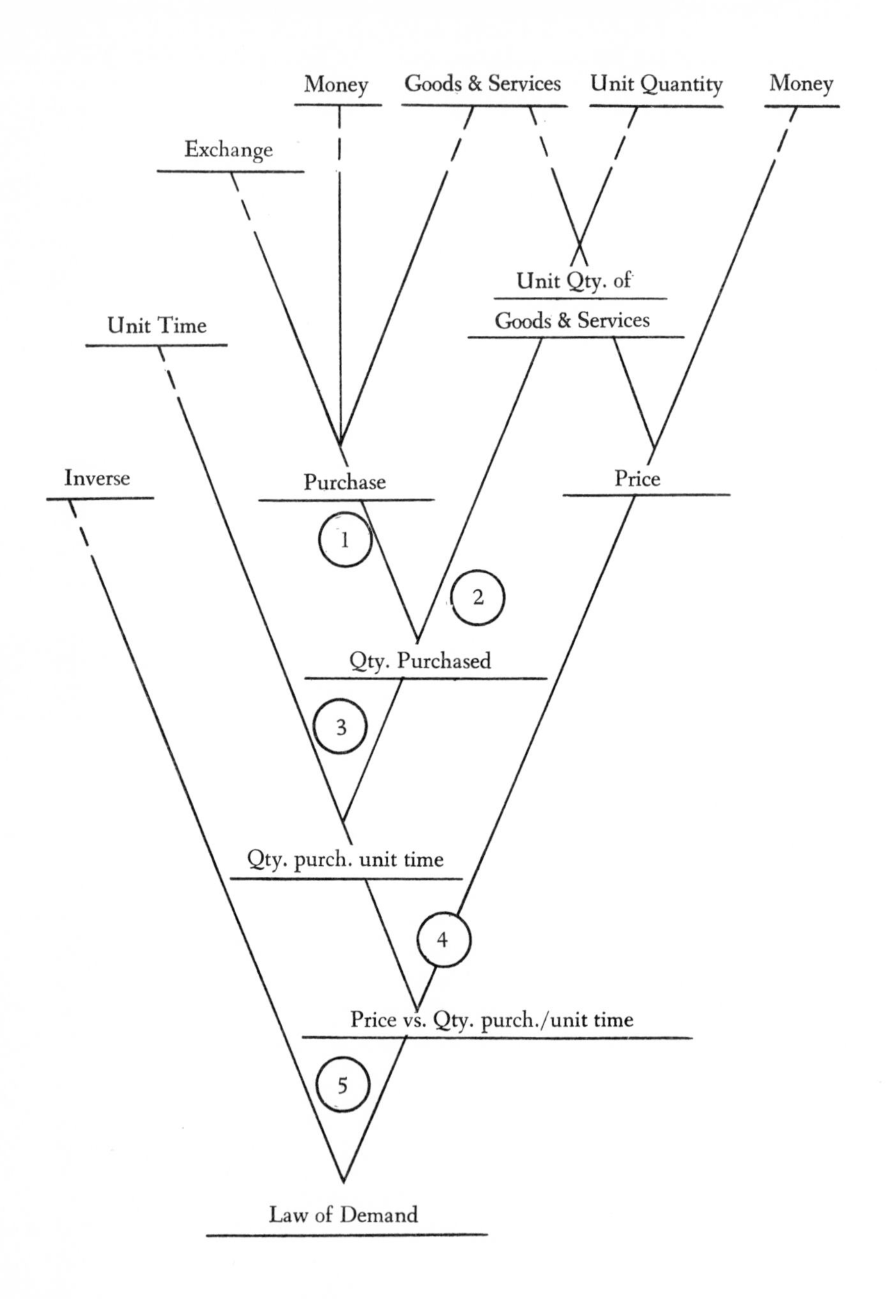

[4] Hickey and Newton (2), p. 15.

quantity" to form "quantity purchases." "Unit quantity" is therefore the second term in the sequence. Tracing the root line to the next node, we pick up the term "unit time," which is combined with "quantity purchased" to form "quantity purchased per unit time." Continuing this procedure, the elemental terms enter the concept in the following sequence:

purchase-unit quantity-unit time-price-inverse-Law of Demand

stimulus elements — response element (concept name)

Although a tree may have some very complex branches, the procedure for ordering the elements can be visualized easily by concentrating on the central "herringbone" pattern.[5]

The herringbone pattern can be seen in the Logic Tree. It shows the order in which the elemental terms enter the growing concept.

It is obvious by now that the sequence of terms entering the major concept, "Law of Demand," could be lengthened by continuously adding sub-chains to simplify any of the very elemental terms. However, the criterion was added to this notion "that all conceptual elements must be delivered without reference to combinations of more rudimentary elements which must themselves be defined."[6] In other words, some "starting points" which are basic and most elemental must be defined, or else the tree would go on indefinitely. Also the basic elements are not used independently in the major concept, but actually are combined to form the sub-concepts. In the Logic Tree in Figure I, the elements—exchange, money, and goods and services—are the basic starting points and assist in forming sub-concepts such as purchase and price. In any use of the Logic Tree an arbitrary decision must be made when a particular term is basic and well understood to be accepted as an element.

From this point in the Logic Tree, the investigators put the tree concepts in a cell matrix for their particular research in programming. Since this discussion is limited to a presentation of major ideas, not particularly to programming alone, no more mention will be made at this time.[7] However, once the Logic Tree, which deals with the concerns of analysis, synthesis, and organization of concepts, is completed, Hickey and Newton move to the other concerns of induction, deduction, abstract, concrete, and so on.

To place these concerns in proper and meaningful order for logical

---

[5] Hickey and Newton (2), pp. 14-16.

[6] *Ibid.*, p. 16.

[7] For a more complete discussion on the programming aspect of this research, see Hickey and Newton (2).

teaching, Hickey and Newton have added another dimension to the Logic Tree to form a "knowledge space" (See Figure II).

Figure II.—A Model of the Logic Space.[8]

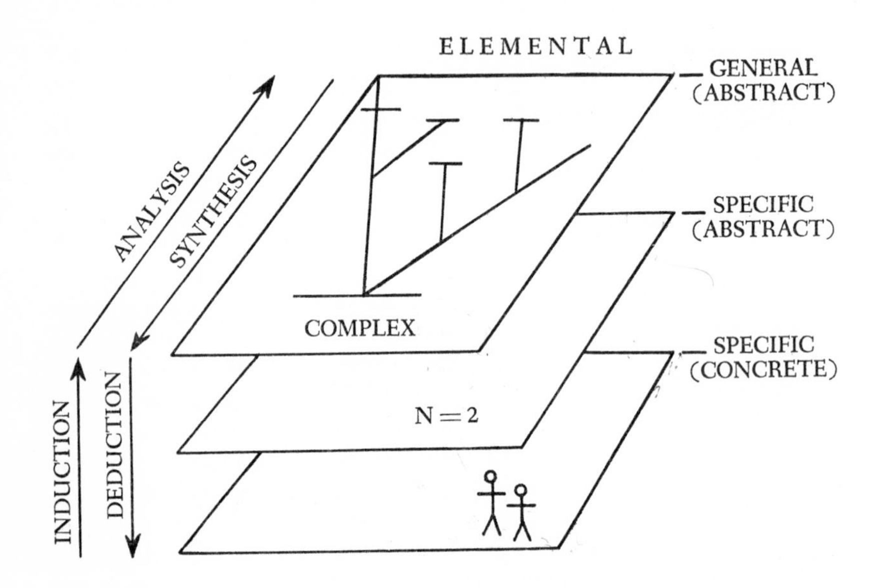

The bottom plane of diagram in Figure II contains concrete, point-at-able events of the real world. Elemental events or phenomena are ranged along the far side of the plane; more complex phenomena (governed by natural laws) are to be found along the near side. Events in this plane are both specific and concrete.

The second plane contains more abstract representations of the specific events to be found in the concrete plane. Thus, the symbol "N = 2" is substituted for the two point-at-able people in the concrete plane. As in the bottom plane, however, the more elemental concepts, such as number, will be found along the far side of the plane, while the more complex phenomena, such as the expression of a function, will be found along the near side.

The top plane contains generalizations of the specific concrete or symbolic examples found on the other two planes. This is necessarily an abstract level. The elemental concepts are again found on the far side, the more complex ones toward the near side.

To progress from the far side to the near side on any plane of the model is to synthesize a phenomenon or concept. To go from front to back is to analyze one. The tree diagram drawn on the top plane shows the logical combination of elements to form a complex concept. The location of a concept on the dimension simple-complex, i.e., its complexity, can be measured by the number of the operations necessary to define or measure it. Thus, in economics, money is a simpler concept than the Law of Demand.

[8] Hickey and Newton (2), p. 8.

> To progress from the bottom or middle plane to the top is to progress from the specific, even concrete, to the general, and necessarily abstract. This is the process of *induction.* To progress from top to bottom is to progress from the general (and abstract) to the specific, the process of *deduction.*
>
> In the vertical concrete-abstract continuum, verbal concepts are at the top, i.e., the abstract or symbolic end. The verbal statement of a principle may, however, correspond to a physical or natural law at the concrete end of the continuum.[9]

Although Hickey and Newton suggest that knowledge can be specified in multi-dimensional terms, they also suggest that knowledge can be taught only in a one-dimensional sequence; the learner can attend to only one thing at a time. They then identify the teaching process as a single thread in the knowledge space and state further that the teacher's problem is one of weaving this single thread up and down and back and forth through this knowledge space. In theory, there are an infinite number of strategies and patterns that can be developed to accomplish this.

At this point, then, some decisions have to be made whether to synthesize or analyze the various elements in the content. Therefore, a conversion from the multi-dimensional space model to a one-dimensional teaching sequence is important and a concern to the teacher. Also, a concept can be taught in very abstract terms or very concrete terms, or perhaps in between. In other words, how can the sub-concepts be attended to—by words, lectures, and/or actual concrete experiences? This is a second concern. A search for teaching sequences is the key process in coping with these concerns.

For the purposes of their research, Hickey and Newton identified twelve alternative sequences of fifty-nine frames for programming the concept of Law of Demand.[10] The twelve alternative sequences varied with respect to three factors: (a) the *direction* of the sequencing, or analysis versus synthesis, (b) the *position* of the frames within the various sub-concepts, and (c) the *order* of the sub-concepts themselves. The effectiveness of each sequence was checked against three criteria: (a) response errors made by the student in the program, (b) speed going through the fifty-nine-frame program, and (c) the transfer of learning measured on a multiple-choice test.

The results of the experiment with the twelve alternative sequences indicated that:

> (a) The sequence variables which were examined did not influence the number of errors made during learning. (b) Faster performance on the program was obtained when the overall program, and all of its parts, began with a statement of the principle being defined and then proceeded to more rudimentary definitions. (c) Students completed the program more quickly when both sub-concepts were learned together rather than separated by the subroutine on basic "market" definitions. However, this effect was most pronounced when "consumption spending" was learned prior to "investment." (d) Students made significantly poorer test scores when learning of both sub-

[9] Hickey and Newton (2), pp. 7-9.

[10] For a good description of the entire research, see Newton and Hickey (3).

concepts was remote from learning the definition of the major concept. However, when the sub-concepts were not learned together, but were separated by the basic definitions, so that one was at the beginning and one at the end of the program, test performance was better if learning of "consumption spending" rather than "investment" was adjacent to learning of GNP [Gross National Product]. This led to the interpretation that "consumption spending" might be the more basic instructional concept in the program.

In brief, the hypothesis that performance is more rapid when principles are stated first was confirmed. The hypothesis that superior transfer would occur when the program proceeded from elements to principles was not confirmed, nor was it rejected. And the hypothesis that sub-concepts might best be learned first and held in storage until needed in the program was generally rejected for this particular program.[11]

Implications for Improved Teacher Education

From this brief description of the experimental and developmental investigation into the field of programmed learning, one can glean some significant meaning for use in teacher education. The effects of programmed learning have caused researchers to give lengthy consideration to the organization and order of the concepts to be learned. The nature of programming is such that the order of teaching events must be structured for effective presentation and learning. Hickey has made this significant attempt in his search for order in content and control of the variables in the cognitive processes.

If one is concerned with the logical order of content to be taught, and desires to organize the particular content in terms of basic elements, sub-concepts, and complex concepts, Hickey's Logic Tree is a helpful model. This organization of content should then provide the teacher with a framework from which to order the elements, sub-concepts, and complex concepts or principles for better teaching and learning. The use of the Logic Tree, therefore, brings to the teaching act an awareness of what is important in the content and affords a pictorial view from which a search for appropriate sequencing of concept teaching can proceed. Although Hickey suggests that some content areas (i.e., mathematics, physics, and economics) lend themselves to this kind of organization better than others, he feels that some significant attempts should be made in other areas. He assumes that there is some degree of structure in a content area.

To search for order and to place content on the tree requires decisions by the teacher. The major concept or principle to be taught, the appropriate sub-concepts, and the basic elements or starting points must be decided upon by the teacher. The tree can then be built from top to bottom or vice-versa, i.e., by analysis or by synthesis. The teacher must identify the concepts and sub-concepts that are important and must be practical in terms of basic elements or starting points. For the starting points, then, the teacher must be aware of the knowledge that his students possess and work from there.

---

[11] Hickey and Newton (2), pp. 53-54.

The Logic Tree model lends itself well to the teaching of a unit of study. For example, if a class were to study the influence of air movements and pressure on weather characteristics in a science class, the logical order might look something like the following:

Figure III.—Influence of Air Movement and Pressure on Weather Characteristics.

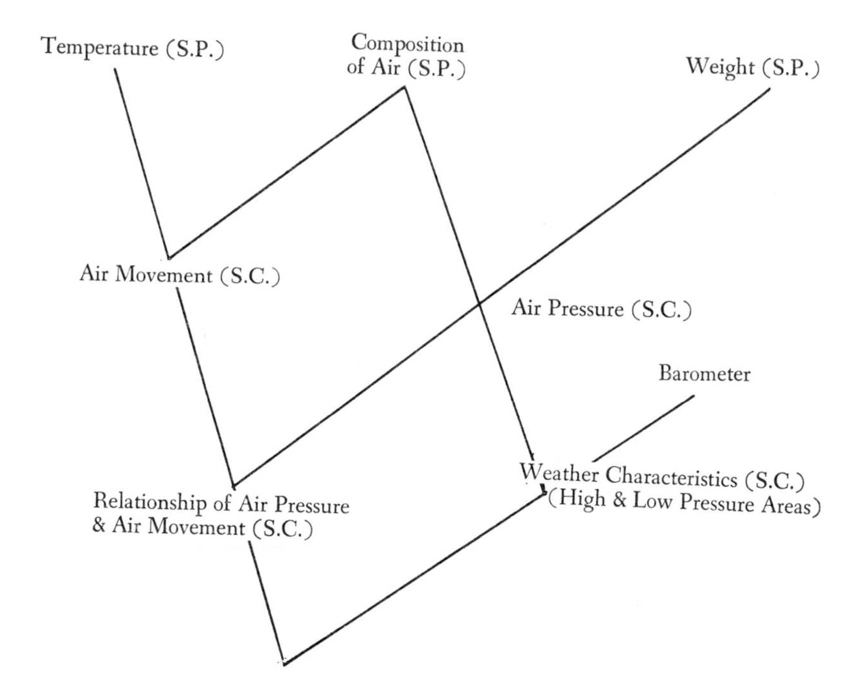

In this simple example, the tree has three starting points (S.P.): a knowledge of the composition of air, a knowledge of weight, and a knowledge of temperature. Then the various sub-concepts (S.C.) are developed along each branch of the Logic Tree. The development of the sub-concepts leads up to the major notion or concept that air movement and pressure influence weather characteristics. Whether this tree is judged correct or incorrect is not particularly important at this time. The important thing is that it provides an order to the content to be taught. Only through developing the sequential order for teaching and actual testing can the tree be judged as valid. In this case, then, it does not dictate methodology, but makes explicit the important aspects of the content under consideration. Hickey suggests that a major weakness in instruction is that not enough thought has been given to the logical structure of the content. The use of the Logic Tree may make some significant inroads into this problem.

The second major contribution of this research to teacher education is, of course, the model on Logic Space which attempts to bring together the important variables in cognitive learning. Hickey places the inductive and deductive processes in this three-dimensional model (which is actually two-dimensional because there is no meaningful horizontal axis for the Logic Tree; although it is depicted in the plane, it is not drawn in cartesian coordinates) with the processes of analysis and synthesis. With the treatment of these processes made explicit, one can easily place for teaching the content which appears in the Logic Tree at the general (abstract) level. From here the actual experiences with the two-dimensional model can be developed.

At the top level generally comes the very abstract meaning such as words, symbols, and the like. At the bottom level comes the very concrete experiences such as experiencing the concept in a real setting. In the middle level Hickey suggests that some simulated experiences could be developed. So within the two levels of the Logic Space model, the teacher should be able to develop the kinds of experiences that will meet the specification of the inductive and deductive reasoning processes and still be free to move back and forth from the elemental to the complex by either synthesis or analysis of the concepts. This model does not tell how to make the teaching moves; it only makes explicit the kinds of experiences needed within the cognitive processes. Decision making by the teacher is necessary within the framework of this model depending on the nature of the content and the students involved.

The teacher education instructor and his students can find considerable meaning at the preservice level from the work of Hickey. Placing the content of an area of study into logical order for teaching should add significant sophistication to the teaching process. It should add to the future teacher's awareness about structuring content and about developing the kinds of experiences needed for cognitive development. It further will permit the student to test the content and process by allowing some experimental sequencing of teaching concepts to occur. The future teacher, upon structuring the Logic Space for an area of study, can test sequences with his students in a laboratory situation. Finally, it will aid the future teacher in the selection of instructional content which is necessary for cognitive growth of his students. These conceptual frameworks can be very important goals for the preservice teacher education student to acquire.

Bibliography

1. ENTELEK. *Programmed Instruction in Economics: Supply and Demand.* Newburyport, Mass.: ENTELEK, 1963.
2. Hickey, Albert E. and Newton, John M. *The Logical Basis of Teaching: I. The Effect of Sub-concept Sequence on Learning.* Final Report to Office of Naval Research, Personnel and Training Branch, Contract Nonr–4215 (00). Newburyport, Mass.: ENTELEK, January 1964.
3. Newton, John M. and Hickey, Albert E. "Sequence Effects in Programmed Learning of a Verbal Concept." *The Journal of Educational Psychology* 56; June 1965.

Chapter 10. Structure of the Intellect

Professor James Gallagher[1] and associates have utilized selected aspects of the model Structure of the Intellect, developed originally by J. P. Guilford of the University of Southern California, for some investigation into the behavior of classroom teachers and students. This chapter will include a brief discussion of the Structure of the Intellect model, Gallagher's application of it, and the meaning of this model and Gallagher's research for improved teacher education.

The three-dimensional cubic model (see Figure I) representing the structure of the intellect has identified a variety of factors that can be ordered, because of similarities, into three different classifications. The first classifying unit is that of the level of operation or processes performed. Within this system are the five major groups of intellectual abilities such as cognition, memory, convergent thinking, divergent thinking, and evaluation.

Cognition, in this case, is the discovery or rediscovery of information and includes comprehension and understanding. *Memory* is the retention or storage of information. From this known and remembered information come the two productive kinds of thinking: divergent thinking and convergent thinking. *Divergent thinking* is the generation of new information from known information with the emphasis on variety and quantity of information. In this case thinking goes in a variety of directions, with no real "right" answer being sought. *Convergent thinking* is the generation of new information which leads to the right or conventionally accepted answer. In this case, the given or known information usually determines the correct response. *Evaluative thinking* is the intellectual process by which judgments and decisions are made regarding the goodness, correctness, adequacy, or suitability of information, based on some criterion of consistency and/or goal satisfaction that resulted from productive thinking.

[1] Dr. Gallagher is Professor of Education and Associate Director of The Institute for Research on Exceptional Children at the University of Illinois.

Figure I.—Structure of Intellect.[2]

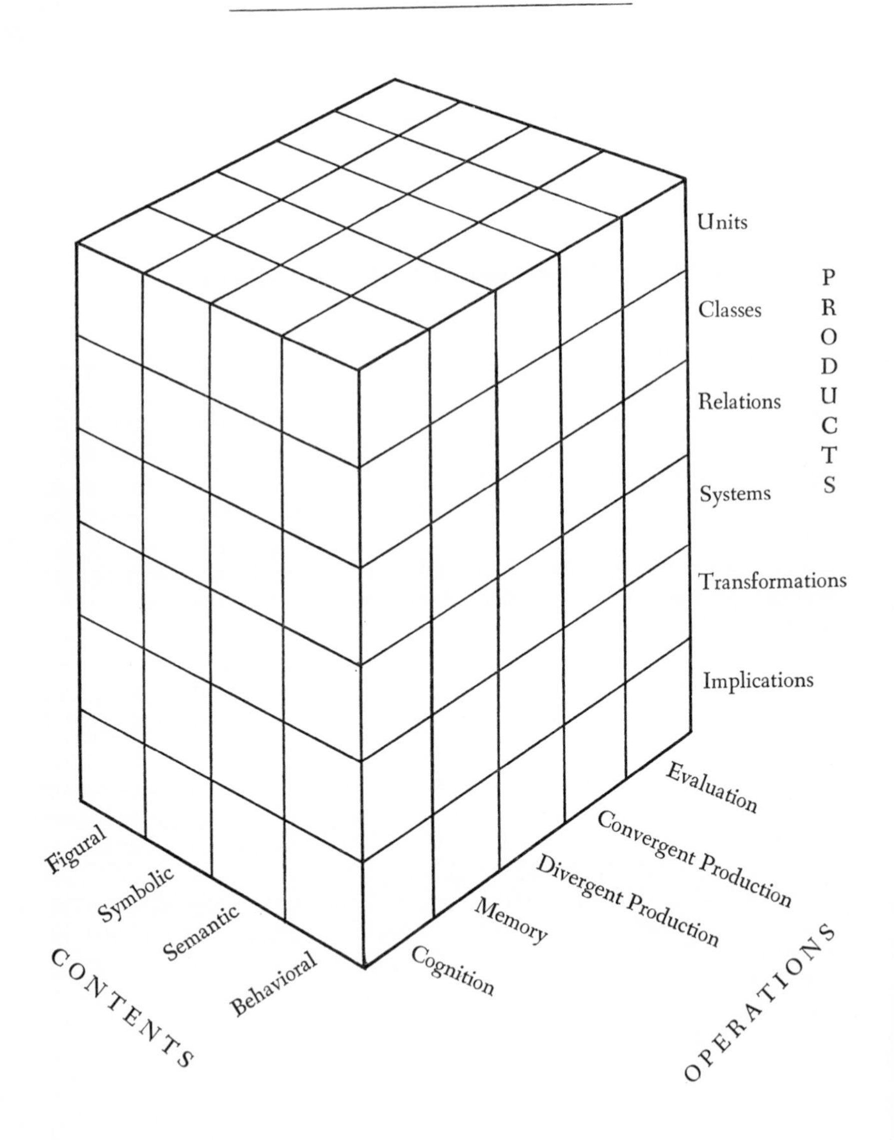

[2] Guilford, Merrifield, and Cox (6).

A second classification system offered in the intellectual process is based on the kind of material or content involved. These broad classes of information are identified as figural, symbolic, semantic, and behavioral content. *Figural content* is that which is concrete material and is represented by itself. This content is taken in through the senses and has some degree of organization. *Symbolic content* is that which is composed of letters, signs, numbers, etc., usually with some organization such as the alphabet or number system. *Semantic content* is information in the form of meanings to which words are attached, and is used primarily in verbal communication. *Behavioral content* is that information, mostly non-verbal, which deals with human interactions in which attitudes, needs, desires, and perceptions of others and oneself are important.

At this point, then, when a certain operation is applied to a selected kind of content, the intellectual process involves a kind of outcome or product. The variety of products involved here are identified as units, classes, relations, systems, transformations, and implications. *Units* are relatively segregated items of information that have a single character. *Classes* are sets of items of information that are grouped by common properties. *Relations* are connections between the units of information based upon certain points of contact that are applicable to them. *Systems* are organized complexes of interrelated or interacting items of information. *Transformations* are the changes in existing, known information or in the actual use of the information. *Implications* are the extrapolations of information, which can take the form of expectancies, predictions, concomitants, or consequences.

From this brief discussion of the factors of the Structure of the Intellect,[3] it can be seen that the intellectual process can be measured in a variety of ways. Guilford developed this model for the specific purpose of testing various kinds of intelligence. From the identification of these factors, it can be seen that 120 possible areas of intelligence should be measured by tests. Gallagher suggests that most standardized tests now measure only memory and convergent thinking and mostly ignore divergent thinking and evaluation.

In addition to the model's use for testing and measuring purposes, its use in the meaningful identification and development of the factors within the intellectual process can lead to other kinds of educational endeavors. It is to this point that Gallagher and associates addressed their attention. They sought to:

1. Identify and classify productive thought processes as expressed by the intellectually gifted children and their teachers in the classroom.
2. Assess relationships between these expressed thought processes and other variables thought to influence their expression in the classroom.[4]

[3] For a more complete discussion, see Guilford (7) or (8).

[4] Gallagher and Jenne (5), p. 2.

Gallagher's basic interest was in the area of productive thinking, and the specific objectives for this research were:

1. To determine if gifted children reveal distinctive individual patterns of cognitive performance in terms of the present Aschner-Gallagher Classification System.
2. To discover whether teachers' cognitive performance is related significantly to variations and patterns in the thought processes expressed by the students.
3. To determine the relationship between attitude and self-concepts and the various thought patterns shown in classroom expressiveness.
4. To determine whether gifted children, who show a high proportion of expressive thought in the classroom, also obtain high scores on tests purporting to measure productive thinking.
5. To determine if there were significant differences between various subgroups of gifted children (such as boys-girls, high divergent-low divergent, expressive-nonexpressive, etc.).
6. To explore the relationships between aspects of family environment and the child's verbal expression in the classroom.[5]

In research involving gifted children at the junior and senior high school level in interaction with teachers, Gallagher utilized the operations dimension of the Guilford model with one exception, that of combining the cognition and memory factors into one. This yielded four categories: cognitive-memory, divergent thinking, convergent thinking, and evaluative thinking. Another category, routine, was added to this system to take care of non-cognitive matters such as giving directions, structuring classes, making assignments, etc. Also within the major category of routine was a sub-category, verdict. This meant giving personal or impersonal praise or reproach to a student or to the entire class. This represented the operational level of the category system used to look at the interaction in the classroom between teacher and students, and more specifically, at teacher and student performance in asking questions (nature of the cognitive task) and responding.

The semantic dimension of the content classification was the only one used in this research because of the concern for verbal behavior of both teacher and student. This provided the well-developed system by which the verbal behavior of the classrooms could be checked.[6]

Prior to the taping of classroom interaction, personality variables were ascertained, Guilford's divergent thinking tests were administered, and family questionnaires were administered. This gave pertinent data about the students involved in the research. Then five consecutive classes conducted by teachers were taped and observed. Some students were involved

---

[5] *Ibid.*, p. 2.

[6] For more complete detail on the category system, see Aschner, Gallagher, *et al.* (1).

in more than one class (i.e., a student in a science class could also be in a social studies or English class).[7]

Some interesting results were obtained from the tape scripts of this extensive investigation into the thought processes as expressed by teachers and gifted students. The most pertinent results of the entire research project are as follows:

1. In terms of total output over the five consecutive class sessions, all teachers showed a predominance of Cognitive-Memory questions. In practically all class sessions, the Cognitive-Memory questions made up 50% or more of the total questions asked. The second most frequently used category was that of Convergent Thinking with much smaller proportions produced by Divergent and Evaluative Thinking questions. In certain class sessions, the requests for the thought operations of divergence and evaluation were absent entirely.

2. An extremely close relationship was obtained between the type of teacher-questions asked and the pattern of thought expression observed from the students' responses. It was clear that the character and style of verbal expression in the classroom was mainly directed by the teacher.

3. Students did not reveal individual differences in patterns of cognitive expression through the major thought categories. While initially, it was felt that some students would specialize in Divergent Thinking and others in Convergent Thinking, this was not found to be the case. The complex nature of thought expression in the classroom in which all major categories had to be used for effective performance, seemed to be responsible for the high intercorrelations obtained on the major categories by the students.

4. Differences were obtained between gifted boys and gifted girls on their degree of classroom expressiveness and on the general attitudes of self and others. The boys tended to be more expressive across *all* measurable dimensions in the classroom and also to show more confidence in their own abilities. The gifted girls appeared to be more positive in their attitudes toward others and expressed a more positive attitude toward the world around them.

5. Since no such sex differences were obtained on tasks of written cognitive ability (in some instances, girls appeared superior) it was concluded that the boy's superiority in verbal expression in the classroom may be related more to personality and attitudinal dimensions than to cognitive ability, especially within the range in the present sample.

6. Expressive teacher differences were obtained over a wide range of secondary categories of verbal expression as well as on such non-cognitive variables as the ratio of positive to negative Verdicts and expressions of Humor.

7. Thought expression, as revealed in teacher questions, seemed to follow a different pattern than those revealed in teacher statements. Teacher questions appeared to represent the teacher's method of advancing class discussions, whereas, teacher statements represented individual cognitive style. Teacher statements remained relatively constant in

[7] For a discussion on specific testing and measuring instruments, personality variables, and interview procedures, see Gallagher and Jenne (5).

style while the type of question varied as the subject was introduced, developed and concluded in class.

8. Comparison of the same student's performance from one point in time to another, and from one subject area to another, showed a significant degree of consistency in general expressiveness.
9. The pattern of performance of the same teacher was observed to vary significantly from one day to another and, in some instances, from one class section to another even while teaching the identical concepts. The total characterization of teacher performance would seem to be very difficult without indicating: (a) the particular group of students with which the teacher is working, (b) the goals of the teacher for this group, or (c) the degree of class progress to these goals at a particular point in time.
10. Performance on Divergent Thinking tests was not related significantly to classroom expressivenesss but did seem to maintain some expected relationships to measures of self concepts and attitudes. In boys, performance on Divergent Thinking tests seemed related to a degree of social independence and autonomy; in the girls, good performance on Divergent Thinking tests seemed more related to a pattern of good academic performance and personal adjustment.
11. Significant differences were found in subgroups in the present study on the basis of cognitive style. An attempt was made to replicate previous work by Getzels & Jackson and Torrance. The results of the present study indicated that teachers rated *Low IQ-High Divergent* boys less well on the cognitive dimension than *High IQ-Low Divergent* boys as would be predicted on the basis of the previous studies. The *High IQ-High Divergent* girls, however, received more favorable teacher ratings and performed more expressively in the classroom than did either the *Low IQ-High Divergent* girls or the *High IQ-Low Divergent* girls. This supported the general conclusion that gifted girls who were superior in IQ and in Divergent Thinking tasks were more self-confident and more expressive in their academic performance.
12. In comparing students who were superior in classroom expressiveness with those inferior in expression in the present sample, differences centered more in the attitudinal dimensions than in the cognitive realm. It was concluded that dependency feelings in the boys may hinder aggressive classroom interaction and be generally related to an academic conformist pattern.
13. For boys, factor analytic procedures failed to reveal any notable relationship between family environment and classroom performance. There was, however, some indication that parental satisfaction with the child's behavior, the child's perception of parental satisfaction, and educational-occupational status of the parents, was related to boys' performance on the Uses and Consequences tests. For *girls,* there was some evidence that family size is related positively to Divergent Thinking performance in the classroom. In addition, for *girls,* there was some evidence that maternal emphasis upon independence-granting, mothers' gainful employment, and stability of parents' marriage were related positively to performance on Uses and Consequences tests. The lack of notable relationships between family environment and child's classroom performance may be due to the relative homogeneity in family background of the children included in this study of classroom performance.

14. It was found that boys whose *fathers* exerted maximum control over their activities (fathers who are both high on achievement-inducing and low on independence-granting) did better in total classroom expressiveness and in divergent production in the classroom than did boys whose fathers indicated less control over activities. It was found that girls with *mothers* who were very high on independence-granting did better in total expressiveness in the classroom than did girls whose mothers were very low on independence-granting.

15. Boys and girls from families in which both parents espoused the Parent-Oriented type of family organization did better in divergent production in the classroom than children from families in which both parents espoused either the Child-Oriented or the Home-Oriented type of family organization.[8]

Some of the conclusions drawn from this extensive study indicated strongly that the teacher is the initiator and determiner of the kinds of thought processes verbalized in the classroom. In other words the teacher generally gets what he asks for in terms of cognitive processes. Since the teacher focuses on the cognitive tasks largely through the kinds of questions asked, questions again loom large in the teaching process.

This research effort again points out vividly the level of thinking required by the teacher for his students. Better than fifty percent of the productive thinking in the classroom was cognitive-memory. Although convergent thinking was present to some degree, very little, if any, divergent thinking and evaluation were present.

These and other conclusions and findings developed from this research have significant implications for the teacher educator and his students. A discussion of these implications, plus those of the use of the model Structure of the Intellect, should again focus some attention on the kinds of thinking taking place that could occur in the classroom.

Implications for Improved Teacher Education

Gallagher suggests that perhaps the Structure of the Intellect model (and the Aschner-Gallagher category system) is too complex for the beginning teacher education student to work with. The model itself is a theoretical system for categorizing the various factors associated with the intellect, and thus is not practical itself. It might be equated with the periodic table found in chemistry and physics. However, like the periodic table, it can be used in part to bring about different combinations at the analytical level for some laboratory teaching.

Gallagher suggests that the operations level—the various kinds of thinking—has particular meaning to the teacher education process. First, the teacher education student can learn how to phrase questions and develop problems for work in a classroom that will elicit a certain kind of cognitive process. A question or problem must, or course, deal with some content and include some implicit outcome. Also, the teacher education

[8] Gallagher and Jenne (5), pp. 6-10.

student should be aware of the instructional purpose associated with the various operations. If an education student desired to work with facts which are important to the other levels of thinking, he would address his attention to the cognitive-memory category. If he were in search for a breadth of possibilities to an area under consideration, or if he were concerned with affective goals such as getting his students to contribute and respond openly, then he would use the divergent thinking category. In this case, he would encourage a building of ideas without criticism or judgment on his part. When all ideas are expended, he can look for immediately usable ideas or economically feasible ideas or most pertinent ideas. An example of this kind of thinking operation might be, How can we improve the automobile? From this question a variety of responses will occur, with judgments held in abeyance until many responses are produced.

If a teacher education student established as his purpose the focusing on a single idea or of bringing to a conclusion some problem, he would use convergent thinking. Finally, at the operations level, if the education student desired to verify or make judgments on some idea, he would use evaluative thinking after, of course, establishing certain criteria.

The exact use of these cognitive operations by the student will develop the analytical behavior desired in the young teacher. From single experiences students can move to more complex operations. It should be obvious that the teaching-learning process will involve a variety of processes. The independence of factors occurs only on the theoretical model, whereas in practical situations the operations are intermixed into a network of classroom activities.

The teacher educator and his students can begin to tie in the operations with specific content in the curriculum. They can frame questions within an area of curriculum that will include productive thinking operations. Some examples are found on the following page.

Finally, in respect to the operations level, the cognitive-memory category should not be slighted. Facts are important. It would be most difficult for a teacher to foster higher level and more productive thinking on the question, Should we get out of the United Nations? if the students have little or no previous knowledge of the United Nations. Therefore, all operations must be considered when working with the future teacher.

Also, Gallagher suggests that the future teacher should become sensitized to the last three categories in the products level—systems, transformations, and implications. The future teacher will assume an active role in the classroom when he strives for these outcomes. Gallagher feels that the first three categories—units, classes, and relations—really don't need too much attention, because they can come quite naturally. The mental products in the last three categories are important and need the attention of the teacher educator and his students.

The research by Gallagher and associates tends to support the notion that more analytical work with operations and products is necessary for the preservice teacher. It was found that questions are important and generally

Examples of Productive Thinking Operations

Subject Area	Divergent Thinking	Convergent Thinking	Evaluative Thinking
Science	How might life be different on Mars?	Explain why there could be no life on Mercury.	Do you think there is life on Mars?
	Name as many possible detrimental effects of the use of insecticides as you can.	How are humans modifying their environment through the use of insecticides?	Are insecticides more harmful or more beneficial?
Social Studies	What would happen if there had not been a Bering Strait?	How did the Bering Strait influence the settlement of North America?	What is the most important contemporary use of the Bering Strait?
	What would have happened if Lewis and Clark had arrived at the mouth of the Frazier River instead of the Columbia?	Explain the impact of the Lewis and Clark expedition on the development of the Oregon Territory.	What were the two most influential contributions of the Lewis and Clark expedition to the development of the Oregon Territory?
Language Arts	Here is the beginning of a short story. How many different endings could be developed from it?	Tell why you think the short story developed in American literature rather than European.	What is more important in the development of the short story — character or plot?
	In what ways has American English changed as a result of advertising?	Explain the impact of advertising on the level of acceptable spoken English.	What kind of advertising made the most valuable contribution in changing American English?

dictate the kind of response received. Further, the comparative paucity of divergent and evaluative thinking seems to indicate that considerable effort should be expended in this area at the preservice level. Finally, the inconsistency of teacher behavior found in this research would suggest some analytic study whereby the teacher can become more aware of the kinds of tasks that he imposes upon his students.

The study and use of the model should assist the future teacher in developing ideas and behavior patterns for better use of cognitive operations, content, and products, and in developing an analytic awareness of classroom operations. This can be considered a most significant goal at the preservice level.

Bibliography

1. Aschner, Mary Jane, and others. *A System for Classifying Thought Processes in the Context of Classroom Verbal Interaction.* Urbana, Illinois: Institute for Research on Exceptional Children, University of Illinois, 1965.

2. Gallagher, J. J., and Aschner, Mary Jane. "A Preliminary Report on Analyses of Classroom Interaction." *Merrill Palmer Quarterly* 9: 183-194; 1963.

3. Gallagher, J. J. "Expressive Thought by Gifted Children in the Classroom." *Language and the Higher Thought Processes.* Edited by R. G. Stauffer. Champaign, Ill.: National Council of Teachers of English, 1965.

4. Gallagher, J. J. "Research on Enhancing Productive Thinking." *Nurturing Individual Potential.* Edited by A. H. Passow. Washington, D. C.: Association for Supervision and Curriculum Development, a department of the National Education Association, 1964. pp. 43-56.

5. Gallagher, James J., with Jenne, William. *Productive Thinking of Gifted Children.* (U. S. Office of Education Cooperative Research Project No. 965) Urbana, Ill.: Institute for Research on Exceptional Children, University of Illinois, 1965.

6. Guilford, J. P., Merrifield, P. R., and Cox, Anna B. *Creative Thinking in Children at the Junior High Level.* (U. S. Office of Education Cooperative Research Project No. 737) Los Angeles: University of Southern California, September 1961.

7. Guilford, J. P. "The Structure of the Intellect." *Psychological Bulletin* 53: 267-291; 1956.

8. Guilford, J. P. "Three Faces of Intellect." *The American Psychologist* 8: 469-479; 1959.

Chapter 11. Inquiry Training

Dr. J. Richard Suchman[1] has done some extensive theorizing and experimenting with elementary school children in the field of scientific inquiry. This chapter will include a discussion and review of the nature of this process, the theoretical model on inquiry, and the necessary components for effective inquiry. The chapter will be concluded with a discussion of the implications of this significant process for improved teacher education.

Suchman's concerns fall within the realm of creativity. He is interested in meaning, or how meaning comes into being for the learner. In other words, how does the learner respond when a new encounter is perceived from the apperceptive masses of stimuli around him? To handle this new encounter, Suchman suggests, the individual has certain organizers which can be drawn upon to bring some meaning to the new encounter. He has identified four organizers as follows: (a) previous ecounters, (b) systems, (c) data, and (d) inferences.

When a new encounter is perceived, the learner can impose some organization by using a previous encounter that was similar in some way. This begins to give meaning to the new event, if nothing more than familiarity. The second type of organizer, systems, helps bring meaning to a new encounter through classification or analysis. For example, the student has a variety of systems for bringing meaning to his classroom. He can categorize the group according to boys and girls, those with glasses and those without, or those who are tall and those who are not. Encounters take on new meaning when systems are applied to them. The systems are thus related to previous encounters, which in turn generate the third organizer, data. Previously stored data can also help bring meaning to a new encounter. In the process of using previous encounters and systems for analyzing and categorizing, the student may infer generalizations, conclusions, theories, etc.—the fourth type of organizer.

[1] Dr. Suchman, a psychologist, was formerly Professor of Education, University of Illinois, and Director of Elementary and Secondary Research, United States Office of Education. He is currently associated with Science Research Associates.

Any one of the four organizers can be stored for future use to give meaning to a new encounter. They can be highly interrelated or quite distinct and inconsistent. If the young elementary child is confronted with a new encounter, for example, the heating and cooling of both sand and water as part of a study of weather, he pulls from storage organizers which bring meaning to these phenomena. Previous encounters help him, for he has probably done some work on heating and cooling. He has a system to talk about heat, cold, and temperture, and a system for measuring with the thermometer. He may have some stored data on heat and cold or water and sand, and thus there is some meaning to the new event. He may have some generalizations stored; for example, heat causes a higher temperature to register than cold, or water will heat faster than sand. These generalizations bring meaning to the new encounter, also. Therefore, as a result of stored organizers, the student can bring some understanding to something that is new. This storage aspect is just one facet of the model of the intellectual process.

Suchman suggests other dimensions to the fact that the youngster is an active system and provides action toward the real world and real things. First of all, the youngster has an intake function which seeks, selects, and groups stimuli coming into his perceptual awareness or things that are happening to him. There is a relationship between the intake stimuli and the student's actions. The student can take action to change the environment or to generate new encounters and thus develop new data.

Since the relationship between intake and action is neither direct nor linear, something must happen between intake and action. Suchman identifies this process as control. The control function plays a crucial mediating role. The student actually does not take action on all intake, nor does he take in all available stimuli at all times. This selectivity points to cognitive filters in the mediation process. This process is most important in inquiring and learning, and Suchman suggests that much more should be known about it.

Finally, the control function is influenced by the motivational state of the learner. Intake selection, retrieval from storage, and action are tuned to serving the needs of the total system as dictated by the motivational function and executed by the control function. Suchman states that the three motivational forces are closure, or the desire to bring to an end the solution or understanding of the particular new encounter; basic curiosity, or excitement about the new encounter; and the power to predict, control, or explain a new encounter.

The above discussion of the inquiry process may be represented schematically, as shown in Figure I. There, the boxes represent functions or processes, and the arrows show the effects of one function upon another.

As is noted in the model, the new encounter comes in through the intake box and then moves through to the mediation or control function. In the control box the decision-making and selectivity begin. Motivational forces begin to work and the retrieval of stored models starts. At this point,

Figure I.—Theoretical Model for the Inquiry Process.[2]

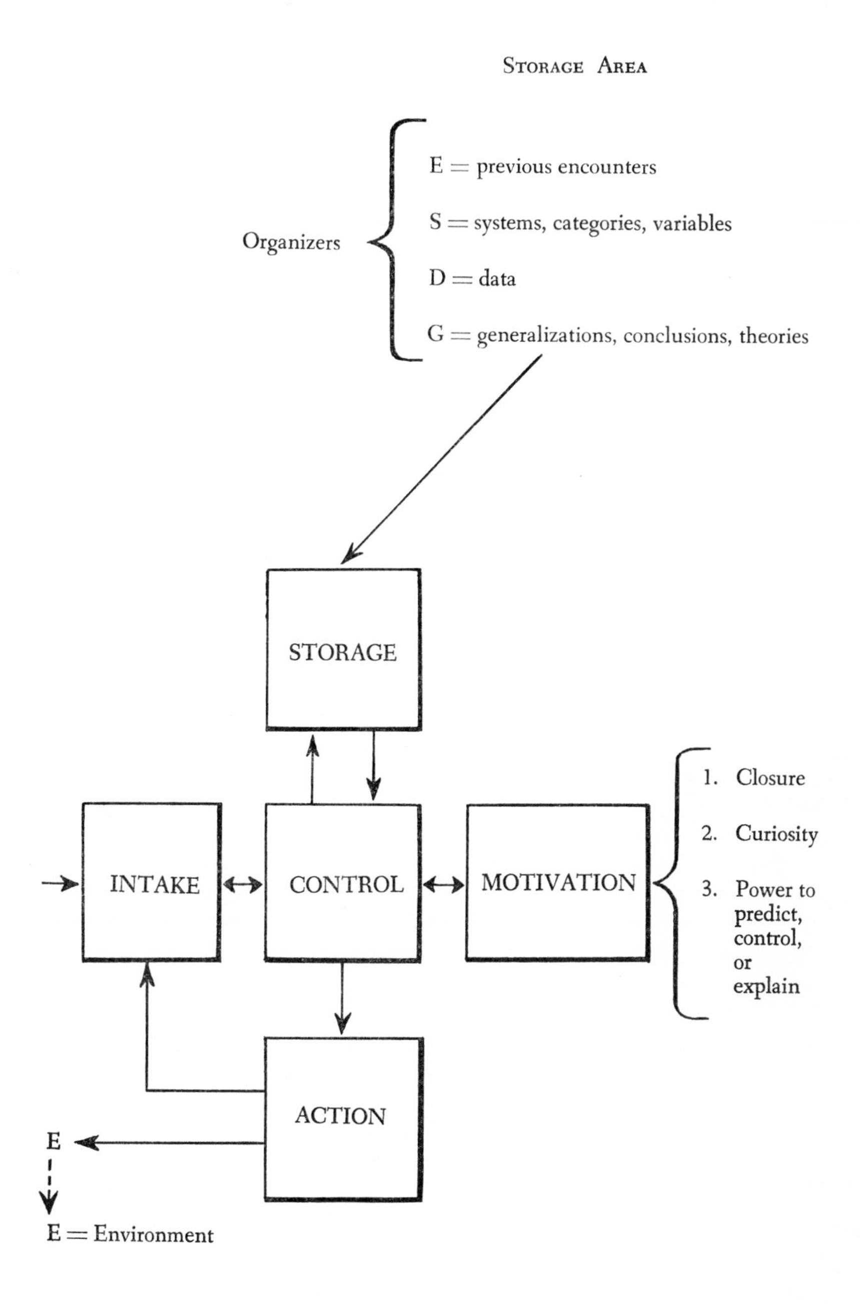

[2] Suchman, from unpublished material

some new data may also be placed in storage. From the control box the decision for action is reached. In this case the action can go to the real world or environment of the individual to help change it, or it can move back to the intake box to generate new stimuli and thus gain more data on the encounter. The cyclical movement is present in the latter case because the learner will keep inquiring until the desired consistency between new encounters and existing structures is obtained.

A brief example of the process, often used by Suchman with his students, can clarify some of the interaction and inquiry associated with this model. When a film on the bimetal strip[3] is shown to students, there usually is a gap in the students' cognitive maps; and they begin to scan their store of organizers to find one that can make this phenomenon meaningful. If no satisfying match can be made between encounter and organizer, dissonance results. The students may then attempt to restructure or combine existing organizers to gain meaning. Suchman argues that when this gap appears, the motivation for closure may be present. At this point the function of the control box is either to perceive the new event so that existing models will assimilate the encounter, or to find some way to combine stored models to create or accommodate a new model.

From here, the students may begin to take action, and because of the dissonance present, they may take action to gather new data and generate intake. Through questions or concrete experiences they can analyze, examine, and test ideas on facets of the bimetal strip. This is done to get models or organizers in storage, such as knowledge about metals or the effect of heat on metals, to assist in developing new meaning. They continue to try out ideas to get new data for the formulation of a new model from parts of old ones. New intake will have meaning from prior intakes and organizers that have been stored. Continued trial and error will occur, then, to get a more meaningful match between intake and storage (or between encounter and organizers), and the cycle is, therefore, present because the students will continue this search for data until the consistency is there. The new data generated will obviously dictate the kinds of organizers used and the kinds that will make sense to the new encounter. This inquiry process will continue until the new encounter has real meaning to the students involved.

The teacher in the classroom should take certain steps to encourage this kind of student inquiry. Suchman suggests that the teacher should:

1. Create freedom to have and express ideas and to test them with data.
2. Provide a responsive environment so that:
   (a) each idea is heard and understood, and
   (b) each learner can get the data he requires.
3. Help learners find a direction to move in, a purpose for their intellectual pursuit.

---

[3] A bimetal strip is a combined metal strip of two dissimilar metals with different coefficients of expansion. Thus, when heated, it bends in only one direction, or toward the metal with the lower coefficient of expansion.

It should be obvious that the first condition is a must for adequate and open inquiry, and that it is the teacher's function to see that the condition is present. The responsive environment is important, for the students must have responses from the teacher when they verbalize their theories or search for new data. The teacher must listen and repeat at times what he thought the students said. Teachers must be responsive to any and all student ideas to encourage inquiry. Also, environmental conditions must be such that the students can gather their data on demand through concrete, simulated, and verbal experiences. Inquiry cannot go on without new data. Finally, teachers must be concerned with focus. If a teacher wants to stimulate and support inquiry, he must direct the cognitive and perceptual energies of students toward some focal point. If this is not the case, diffuse behavior may occur with little or no satisfaction resulting for students. The teacher can inject focusers, such as a film on the bimetal strip, to mobilize the energies of the students to inquire. Also, the teacher may want to refocus attention when inquiry stops because of premature closure. If, for example, students close quickly on the bimetal strip phenomenon by stating flatly that the heat causes the bend, the teacher should refocus by asking why it bends one way on some occasions and the other way on other occasions even though heat is being applied during both experiments. This refocusing will then expose a discrepancy, which will promote more inquiry. Suchman states that some children will refocus by themselves for the sake of deeper meaning or for the excitement of pursuing it.

At this point it might be instructive to compare the inquiry mode with the didactic function of the teacher in which he takes the major responsibility for engineering learning, particularly conceptual growth. The teacher can use language to influence the control center to retrieve from storage selected organizers for interpreting an encounter. Through words, stored models are retrieved, tried out, and perhaps held in abeyance if they are not compatible with the new encounter. Through continued interaction, other stored models are brought out. The teacher may use graphic or schematic models on the board in conjunction with the stored models. This assists the students in restructuring to search for the new, consistent model which, in turn, may lead to generating new encounters.

The teacher in this case has moved to influence the control box and has regulated its activity with language. This, in turn, has caused some internal restructuring within the student. The teacher, therefore, can engineer the buildup of new models out of old ones using language, symbolic systems like graphs, and deliberately introduced encounters, when needed. This is truly teacher-planned and teacher-engineered learning. The teacher may try to deal with each encounter in the light of the model that he is trying to develop. Further, the teacher must check to see if the model that the student is using, related to the new encounter, is the one that the teacher had in mind. This means that some sampling device or feedback is most necessary. Without this feedback, the student could go in much different directions than desired. From the feedback, the teacher assists the student at the action level either to test his new model on the encounter, or to go back to the intake box for new data for continued restructuring of existing models. The activity itself is the student's. The teacher is not giving him new knowledge or ideas. The teacher influences the sequence and direction of activity. Learning certainly can take place under these conditions, but this does not mean the pupil will learn about inquiry or how to inquire. Good didactics will always have a place in education, but it is not everything, Suchman claims.

One can begin to glean the importance of the above theoretical discussion[4] on the inquiry process for the teacher education program and student.

Implications for Improved Teacher Education

The goals subscribed to by Suchman and his inquiry process are most consistent with current educational thought. Inquiry with experimentation, investigation, discovery, and thinking are processes that hold real meaning for education today, and probably will for some time. Therefore, the meaning of the inquiry process developed by Suchman has particular importance at this time. The teacher of tomorrow should have an awareness and a working knowledge of this important process. The preservice teacher should examine carefully what is meant by meaning[5] and new encounters, and how to evolve these in his teaching process. Further, asking questions and responding to students are important facets of the inquiry process that should be understood and used by the preservice student. Finally, the act of focusing and refocusing on problems at hand are important operations that the student must know. The teacher education student must also have a good knowledge of the content that will be taught to enable him to develop the appropriate experiences and materials for true inquiry.

Although Suchman has confined his experimentation into the inquiry process primarily to elementary school children, this process can be used at any level of education. Therefore, an awareness of the process and experience using it should come at the teacher education preparatory level. A basic understanding of the theoretical model and its functions, the awareness of the requirements necessary for active and meaningful inquiry, and the understanding of the role[6] that the teacher must play to enhance inquiry are important factors for teacher educators to consider in their programming of experiences. Suchman suggests that since inquiry produces learning, the teacher education student should inquire into the nature of students, curriculum,[7] and the teaching-learning process. There is no better

---

[4] For a complete discussion and kit on the actual operations and materials necessary for the inquiry process, see Suchman (3).

[5] For more discussion on meaning, see Suchman (2).

[6] For more discussion on the role of the teacher, see Suchman (6).

[7] For a discussion on inquiry and the curriculum, see Suchman (4).

way to learn about inquiry than to inquire and then analyze what has been done. Opportunities for inquiry into the behavior of public school students, the way in which students learn, the means of developing materials, and actual operations of the classroom must be present for the teacher education student. They provide the new encounters in the inquiry process. The teacher education student can find out or experience the actual inquiry about the entire classroom himself. Follow-up discussions with the instructor and the exchange of experiences with others will then help the student to start developing the consistent models necessary for effective inquiry. Instruction through readings and other experiences plus the continued experiencing of the actual classroom operations (new intake) will continue the process of effective model building. In this teacher education process the instructor must continue to supply new organizers for the student until the models on teaching and learning desired by the instructor are consistent with his student's models.

This process, of course, is far different from existing ones on teacher education where primarily untried models are given to the student for storage only. However, this development of appropriate behavior through actual experiencing is most important. Suchman states that the inquiry process affords an openness for continued learning and inquiry by the future teacher. Few teacher educators would argue against this goal.

Bibliography

1. Suchman, J. Richard. *Developing Inquiry.* Chicago, Ill.: Science Research Associates, 1966.

2. ———. "In Pursuit of Meaning." *The Instructor* 75: 32+; September 1965.

3. ———. *Inquiry Development Program in Physical Science.* Chicago, Ill.: Science Research Associates.

   A kit including teacher demonstrations and student experimentation materials, a record on inquiry, several pamphlet guides, films, and a booklet on developing inquiry for direct use in a classroom with children in the area of physical science.

4. ———. "Inquiry in the Curriculum." *The Instructor* 75: 24+; January 1966.

5. ———. *The Elementary School Training Program in Scientific Inquiry.* (U. S. Office of Education Title VII Project No. 216) Urbana, Ill.: University of Illinois, January 1964.

6. ———. "The Role of the Teacher." *The Instructor* 75: 26+; December 1965.

Chapter 12. Concept Formation and Learning Unit Design

Asahel Woodruff[1] has devoted considerable thought and developmental effort in the area of basic concept formation and the meaning it has for behavior and learning. As a result he has considered the design of units for effective learning and concept formation. This chapter will include a discussion of concept formation, as defined by Woodruff, and unit design. The implications of these important functions for improved teacher education will conclude this chapter.

Concept Formation

Woodruff defines the term concept as follows:

> *General definition of a concept*—A concept is a relatively complete and meaningful idea in the mind of a person. It is an understanding of something. It is his own subjective product of his way of making meaning of things he has seen or otherwise perceived in his experiences. At its most concrete level it is likely to be a mental image of some actual object or event the person has seen. At its most abstract and complex level it is a synthesis of a number of conclusions he has drawn about his experience with particular things.[2]

Using this definition of concept formation, Wodruff suggests that a conceptual statement in a form which is useful for planning a unit of instruction is: "A description of the properties of a process, structure, or quality stated in a form which indicates what has to be demonstrated or portrayed so a learner can perceive the process, structure or quality for himself."[3]

In this case, then, Woodruff has identified three kinds of concepts:

---

[1] Dr. Woodruff is Professor of Education at the University of Utah.

[2] Woodruff (3).

[3] *Ibid.*

process, structural, and quality. Definitions and examples of these three kinds of concepts are as follows:

> *Process concepts*—A concept of a process, event or behavior and the consequences it produces when it occurs. A statement of this kind should take this form:

When	this or these	event(s) process(es) behavior(s)	occur(s)	it they	will tend to pro- duce	this result or these feelings or these conditions or these reactions.
		circumstance(s) quality(ies) structure(s)	exist(s)			

Example: When a person acts adjustively, the concepts and value judgments which mediated the act are empirically tested by the consequences of the act, and the ensuing perceived results either modify or reinforce the concept or value.

> *Structural concepts*—A concept of an object, relationship or structure of some kind. A statement of this kind should take this form:

This	quality process object idea condition place organization etc.	has these elements	height depth width number substance motion time units etc.	in this	form structure configuration.

Example: The verbal processes of instruction may deal with the (a) parts of a referent, (b) functions of a referent, (c) characteristics or qualities of a referent, and/or (d) the way a referent develops in assisting the learner in the formation of concepts.

> *Quality concepts*—A quality is a property of an object or process and has no independent existence. Nevertheless, we speak of qualities as if they had independent existence, by abstracting them or taking them out of objects or processes in which they are found and by treating them in the abstract. However, qualities operate in our thinking in the same way as structures and processes. We see them as structural entities, or we see them as processes having certain effects. "Square" is an abstract structural concept. "Kind" is an abstract process concept.[4]

With these basic definitions in mind, the attention can be turned to Woodruff's basic cybernetic model, "The Cognitive Cycle in Behavior and Learning" in Figure I. This extensive model is divided into two sections for discussion purposes.

---

[4] *Ibid.*

Figure I.—The Cognitive Cycle in Behavior and Learning with Forms of Conceptual Elements Located in Relation to the Decision-Making Process.[5]

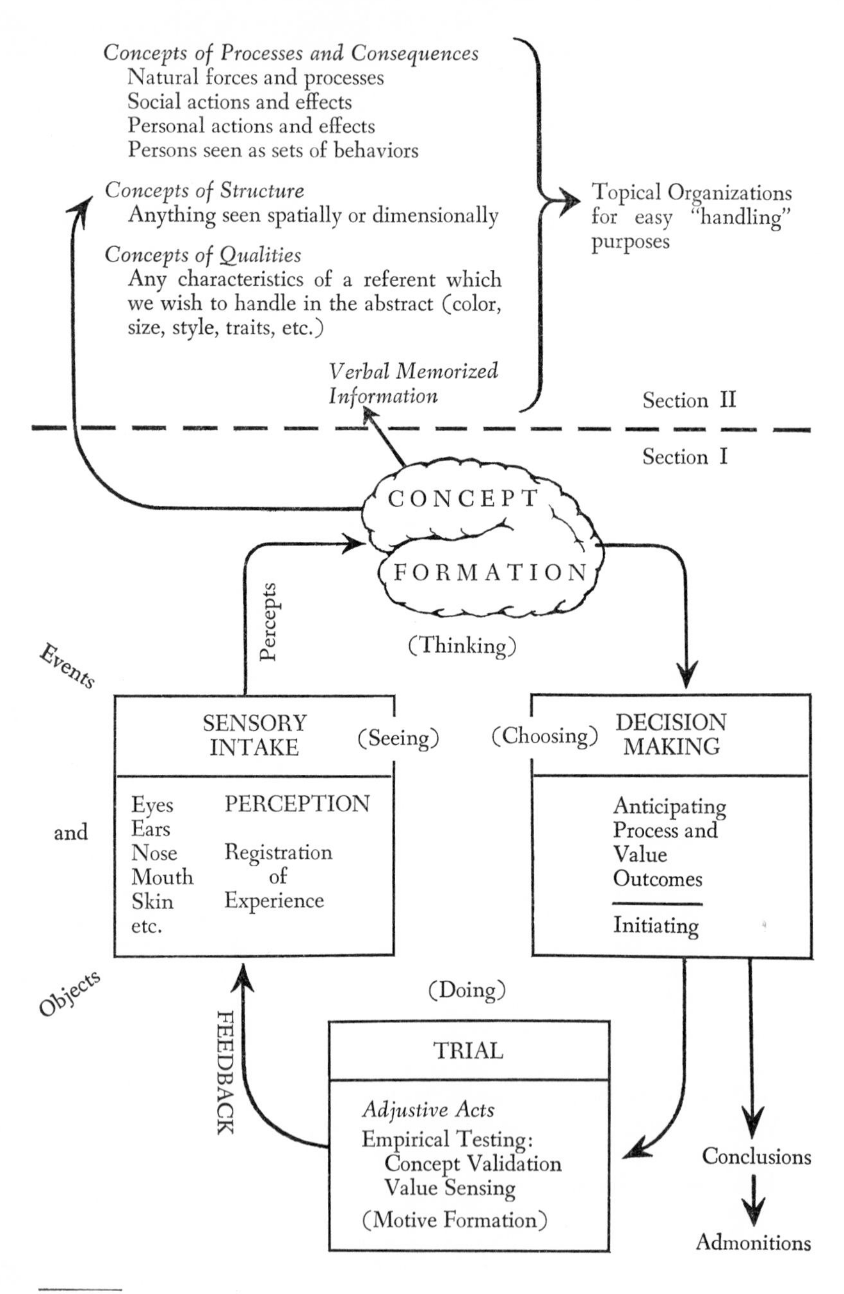

[5] Woodruff (3).

The verbal statement (structural concept) for the lower part of the model (Section I) would be as follows:

> Human behavior and learning operate in a cycle beginning with referential-perception input and followed by assimilation, accommodation, try-out, and feedback to referential-perception input. Conclusions are products of decisions, and admonitions are derivations from conclusions.

The organization of the upper part of Figure I (Section II) may be described as follows:

Cognitive meanings take several forms in the brain, each having a different potential for decision-making process or behavior.

1. Percepts (the sensory beginnings of concepts).
2. Concepts (organized perceptions; the elements from which decisions are made) are of three kinds:
   a. Processes—a concept of a process, event, or behavior and the consequences it produces when it occurs.
   b. Structures—a concept of an object, relationship, or structure of some kind.
   c. Qualities—a quality is a property of an object or process and has no independent existence.
3. Derivations from conceptual knowledge.
   a. Topics—categories of knowledge for "filing" purposes.
   b. Data—items of information (verbal form) related to concepts.
   c. Definitions of terms—condensed and generalized concepts.[6]

Woodruff states that this model of learning and behavior is much like a computer, because there is energy input, in fact a complete energy system, thus the term cybernetic. Input of perceptions enters through the senses from the real world outside to the brain system. They are held in storage at the beginning, but these bits of perceptions begin to become associated in time as they relate to meaning from the past. As the meanings from these bits of past perceptions become associated with one another they form concepts. The concepts at this stage can be either large or small, complete or incomplete, specific or general, or concrete or abstract ideas. However, as these concepts accumulate, they begin to act as mediating variables, which means they are inside the organism between the intake stimuli and the responses that come from them; they (in turn mediate to) shape the behavior of the individual.

The move is thus made from the concept formation stage to the decision-making one. Decision-making is choosing on the basis of accumulated ideas. The person looks at the new situation and makes a decision which is harmonious with and produced by stored concepts, and out of this kind of mediation emerges the next stage of the trial or adjustive act. This is the way the individual meets the situation that has stimulated him.

Through this trial performance the individual is putting his ideas to a test in operation, which involves him in consequences. The consequences

[6] *Ibid.*

in turn cause a feedback to occur, and as a result of the feedback there is an entering of percepts into the system again. Therefore, the entire system is cyclical in nature, with new percepts coming in to form concepts, which in turn are acted upon by the decision-making and trial process and feedback.

This cognitive cycle will continue to function until the situation with which the individual is confronted is harmonious with the concepts that the individual possesses. In this case ideas give rise to behavior, which gives rise to fresh input and alters the ideas. Woodruff suggests that this can be called natural empirical learning. This is the kind of learning that a person goes through in his experiences at work, in the neighborhood, and at home. The individual learns as he goes along, finding that concepts control behavior in the making of decisions. Decisions lead to acts and acts to consequences. The consequences then lead to fresh input and an alteration of ideas. In everyday learning outside the school the cycle goes around and around.

With this model kept in mind, Woodruff states that there is no such thing as learning in any real sense. There is nothing but behavior, and behavior changes while it is going on. Learning, therefore, is a change in behavior. This requires an experience-centered learning curriculum, which, Woodruff argues, is not present to any great extent in schools today. The curriculum currently is concerned mostly with symbolic knowledge. He believes it is a fundamental error to assume that the normal cycle of behavior can be suspended in school while a massive verbal exercise is carried on, with the expectation that this exercise can somehow alter the behavior which occurs when the normal cycle is again permitted to operate.

In terms of the meaning knowledge has for the cognitive cycle, Woodruff suggests that knowledge is about the "real world." The real world consists of objects which are engaged in events which have consequences that impinge upon the self and affect its sense of well being. Therefore, the five component elements that constitute the significant aspects of environment as far as learning is concerned are: (a) objects that are around an individual, (b) the events in which the objects take part, (c) the consequences of those events, (d) how they impinge upon him, and (e) how he feels about them. These five kinds of concepts are the ones that will be forming in the mind of the individual.

Since these are the important concepts in learning, consideration must be given to how they are formed. Concrete or real things must be taken in through the perceptual organs where they are registered. This concrete form can be referred to as a mental image of objects, and quite naturally is a derivative of looking at specific objects and events. The individual begins to do things with these concrete concepts. He starts to associate and combine them imaginatively and mold them into different kinds of abstractions, generalizations, and principles. Perhaps the most important consequence of combining concrete concepts is that it helps the individual to predict what is going to happen. These are termed predictive variables by Woodruff.

Further, this is what a concept is used for in human behavior: to predict what is going to happen.

At this stage they become mental constructs, rather than mental images, because there is nothing out in the real world like the mental constructs possessed by the individual. These mental constructs give rise to generalized object categories or functionally related sets of events which are seen as total processes with their consequences, and this in turn gives rise to principles and abstract concepts. This permits the individual to make predictions.

As these concepts are continually forming, the individual can verbalize them in either written or oral form. Woodruff suggests that this is still conceptual knowledge, but now it is being expressed verbally. He sees conceptual knowledge and verbal knowledge as being distinctly different, resulting from different kinds of input and storage. Verbal expression of concepts does not make them verbal knowledge. Verbal knowledge consists of "memorized" data, such as figures, names, dates, words, and paragraphs learned without meaning.

Woodruff also suggests that in certain subjects which have extensive symbol systems, an individual can skip steps from one idea to another by using symbolic strategies, such as logic or statistics, and still arrive at a valid conclusion. However, this can be done only after the concepts have been formed through the above stages. Every subject can be expressed in a *verbal* symbolic system, but this does not necessarily lead to the use of symbol *strategies*. As long as there is a one-to-one relationship between a word and a concept, all that is going on is communication. However, a field such as mathematics has, in addition to its quantitative referents and the concepts acquired from them, a separate symbol system which is nonverbal. The system can be referred to verbally, but what actually is referred to is a set of "numerals" (not numbers) and their relationship within the symbol system. It is the systematic movement through that system that constitutes the symbol strategy. The system is internally tight and logical and can be studied as a phenomenon without reference to real numbers and objects. One can learn this form of mathematics without possessing the concepts of numbers.

Finally, Woodruff suggests that mostly verbal and symbolic knowledge is used in our public schools today. Of course, concepts cannot be formed without first having concrete images. Young people must perceive real things first, then make their own concepts. This is conceptual knowledge—the input of real things and their transformation into conceptual structures. Therefore, real things must come in through perceptual senses, not through language. Language is only a form of expressing one's knowledge. It can function as a stimulating and suggestive influence on a learner as he forms his concepts, but not as a substitute for perception.

Learning Unit Design

From the development of ideas on basic concept formation, Woodruff moves to the important characteristics of an effective instructional unit which are consistent with and can accomplish the features of adequate concept formation.

In the most complete sense, instruction is aimed at changing behavior. Therefore, every act of instruction is assumed to be pointed at some behavioral act. For that reason it is helpful to think of a unit of instruction as being built around a terminal behavior.

Behavioral acts obviously vary in size and complexity. Some are very simple and specific, largely reflexive in form, such as those that meet the criteria of classical conditioning, which Robert Gagné calls "Signal Learning" (Type 1). Some meet the criteria for "operants" (Gagné's Type 2) and seem to be acquired by operant conditioning. Concepts do not seem to be significant variables in these limited behaviors; but on up the scale of complexity they become increasingly important, and then decisively determinant.

Woodruff sees a need for conditioning some behavior. Some processes require no logical conceptual content for their acquisition, and conditioning is the best way to effect this behavior. An example of terminal behavior is the act of performing multiplication of three-digit numbers by two-digit numbers within ten seconds. Another example might be grammatical expression to be used in the classroom. There is no logic to this learning, so the terminal behavior is conditioned.

The learning tasks of the school involve some operants, but consist mostly of more complex behaviors which require extensive conceptual learning. To keep the conceptual content seminal, however, it is well to build the curriculum around the behaviors we wish to produce and select concepts which are required to produce those behaviors. Thus the suggested form of an instructional unit is that of a terminal behavior and all of the subordinate concepts, operants, symbolic data, and vocabulary required to produce it.

Without discounting the importance of operant conditioning, Woodruff limited his attention in the work under discussion primarily to conceptual learning, since teachers frequently will be required to plan and carry out supplementary instructional units for a single concept objective.

According to the cognitive cycle the subject matter for any concept automatically becomes the objects, events, and consequences that are taken in through the sensory organs. This perceptual process is the beginning of concept formation. Behavior that is mediated by concepts cannot be conditioned. The exacting conditions required in the cognitive cycle must be met in order to achieve concept formation. An example of a process concept is found in this propositional statement: "When dissipative forces are increased, matter tends toward the gaseous state."[7] Input of percepts,

[7] Woodruff (2).

internal organizing of what is perceived, decision-making, trial, and feedback will be required to form this concept and mature it. An example of a structure or object is found in this description of a fugue: "A fugue contains a theme, repeated many times, and carried by several different voices in a non-simultaneous arrangement, with the repetitions phased so as to maintain both harmony and balance throughout the composition."[8] Such a construct can be conceived only if it has some actual experience with the elements included in the construct.

Thus, the instructional unit is designed according to the outcome desired, whether it be a terminal behavior directly or the acquisition of a concept or concepts. If one chooses the terminal behavior to be produced by conditioning processes, Woodruff suggests that the unit should specify both the capabilities to be acquired during the instruction and the prerequisite capabilities required before the instruction begins. Then there should be a sequence for the conditioning experiences to be used to reach the terminal behavior. This is all that is necessary.

In the second operation of building concepts a much different approach is needed. This unit should include a concept statement which identifies all of the components contained in the concept. Therefore, the content is not something to be selected; it is derived from the concept to be acquired. The purpose in writing the concept statement is to identify the content. In the process concept example (on gases and forces) stated above, the content is dictated by the nature of the concept. In this case, the content would have to deal with gases and forces and how they interact. This entire idea of the relationship of concept to content is quite different from present curriculum construction practices, but for the adequate formation of concepts according to Woodruff's cognitive cycle, this must be the case—concepts dictate content.

Proceeding with his discussion of unit design for concept formation Woodruff states that conceptual objectives exist in a hierarchy or sequential taxonomy (see Figure II). At the lower or beginning end is the process of perception, operating on specific and concrete objects and events in nature. These are the basic subject matter for the whole curriculum.

The starting point of Figure II is identification. This is where the sensory percepts are taken into the cognitive cycle; therefore, referential material is needed. It should be noted that this step in the unit plan can be omitted if prior identification of phenomena has been accomplished. From here the differentiation process takes effect to determine with more precise perception the nature of the phenomena and to find important characteristics.

Woodruff divides the conceptual objectives at this point into the process concepts and structural or object concepts. The process objects are given considerable importance by Woodruff, because these are the ones that truly affect behavior and behavioral change. The structure concepts

[8] *Ibid.*

Figure II.—Hierarchy of Conceptual Objectives.[9]

(e) FORMATION OF A PRINCIPLE

Assumes a repertoire of specific instances of a process and its consequences, and requires discovery of invariable relationships among them

(d) RECOGNITION OF VALUE

Assumes concepts of processes and consequences, and requires perception of how people feel about the consequences

(d) FORMING MORE GENERAL GROUPS

Assumes awareness of pervasive common characteristics and their differentiation from irrelevant differential characteristics

(c) FORMING OF PROCESS CONCEPTS

(i) NATURAL PROCESSES AND PROCEDURES

(ii) TECHNICAL PROCESSES TO ASSIST LEARNING OR TO GUIDE THE FORMING OF A CONCLUSION OR DECISION

Analysis
Synthesis
Evaluation
Problem solving
Self-directed learning

Assumes identification of a class of events and the consequences they consistently produce

(c) FORMING A CLASS CONCEPT (GENERAL)

Assumes differentiation of characteristics to be used for classifying objects or events

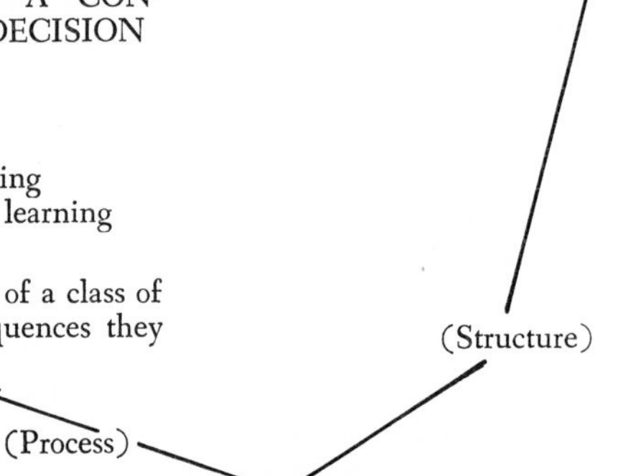

(b) DIFFERENTIATION

Assumes identification, and requires more precise perceptions to find differentiating characteristics

(a) INDENTIFICATION

Assumes no prior learning, but requires sensory ability to perceive, and referential materials to be perceived

[9] Woodruff (2)

play a secondary role. Moving up the ladder of process concepts, three other considerations are necessary.

First, the formation of process concepts by the natural processes and procedures defined in Woodruff's cognitive cycle or by such technical processes as forming conclusions through analysis or synthesis is necessary. Through this concept formation activity, concepts of processes and consequences are formed. As the consequences are perceived, the perception of how one feels about the consequences also takes place. Woodruff identifies this as the recognition-of-value level, and he points out that this value idea is gained at the same time the process concept is formed. This means, then, that the affective and cognitive elements of a concept are formed at the same time. The formation of the principle occurs next in the process concept. This is where the variable relationships of specific instances of a process and its consequences are formed. The formation of process concepts, then, has the power to effect behavior of the individual, for behavior is essentially the use of processes.

Moving up the hierarchy on the right-hand or structure concept side, the classification of objects or events occurs after the differentiation of characteristics is completed. Classifying is essentially the forming of more general groups. As an example, structural concepts building about dogs in general might begin upon perceiving both cats and dogs. First the differentiation takes place, then the classifying of characteristics of dogs. Finally a general group called dogs is formed by viewing common characteristics and their general differentiation from both irrelevant differential characteristics and the characteristics of cats.

Any level in this hierarchy can be used if the following criteria are satisfied: (a) The behavior to be attained, or the concept to be acquired, is stated clearly, precisely, and completely. (b) The prerequisite competencies or concepts are identified and are present in the learner. (c) The sequence of appropriate experiences is specified to lead from the prerequisite competencies to the target behavior or concept.[10]

Other considerations for designing an instructional unit are advanced by Woodruff. He suggests that the unit should indicate how the referential elements will be brought into focus for learning, that is, how the teacher will bring to the students the elements for initial perception. This requires a decision, because the student may have enough input present in storage so that he may not require a perceptual process. Then he can proceed with a concept organizing process. Of course, the reverse, no previous input, could be possible. In that case adequate perception must be supplied. An inventory by the teacher should determine the case.

If the elements have not been adequately perceived before, the unit should indicate the sequence in which they are to be shown, media and materials to be used, and directions to be provided to guide the learner's attention. The nature of the cognitive cycle expressed by Woodruff

[10] *Ibid.*

(Figure I) should be observed closely for this introduction of basic elements to students.

If, however, the percepts or sub-concepts used in forming the new concept are already internalized by the learner, the unit should provide for their recall and review by furnishing appropriate stimuli to evoke recall and by providing an organizing focus for selecting relevant components and assembling them. This can be done through appropriate verbal statements and the use of selected media and materials. Further, Woodruff suggests that this can be accomplished by providing ways of using the newly formed concept to activate the empirical cycle of learning. The unit, then, should provide a response-requiring situation in which the new concept is relevant and in which the learner's adjustment will be affected by his responses. It should also require the learner to make a decision using his concept and act on it. Finally, it should help him interpret the consequences, related both to meaning and to value. All of the statements in this paragraph should cause the reader to review Woodruff's notions on basic concept formation again, because designing the learning unit follows the statements on concept formation.

The next step in designing the unit requires that it contain a calculated balance between referential input and interpretive discussion, as appropriate to the readiness of the learner. Woodruff sees four possible alternatives here. First, learning may begin on the perceptual level and stay there to produce identification and differentiation only. Second, learning may begin on the perceptual level and move to an organizing level through discussion. Third, learning may begin on the organizing level, using only percepts and sub-concepts already present in the learner. Or fourth, learning may shuttle between the two levels when new percepts are needed to support or suggest organizing ideas. Again, designing the unit requires decisions by the teacher concerning the readiness of the student and the level at which learning should begin.

In the next step, Woodruff suggests that the unit include teaching strategies and verbal patterns that the teacher can use to stimulate the acquisition of appropriate levels of meaningfulness by the learner. The levels of meaningfulness are those found in Figure II: indentification, differentiation, forming concepts of processes and their consequences (from simple to complex), forming concepts of possible goals and their relative values, forming concepts of principles, forming concepts of general classes of objects or events (simple or complex), and forming concepts of special technical processes one may use to improve the quality of the learner's mental activities (i.e., analysis, synthesis, and evaluation). Since the learner should experience these levels of meaningfulness in the process of concept formation, the strategies and verbal patterns are most important. Woodruff suggests that some strategies for this area of unit designing would be found in the work by Smith (Chapter 2), Bellack (Chapter 6), and Taba (Chapter 3). For verbal interaction patterns, see Flanders (Chapter 5) and Gallagher (Chapter 10).

The next step in designing a unit is to designate the imput of symbolic materials to be memorized. The input of symbolic materials should be restricted to: (a) vocabulary related to the concept, (b) non-verbal signs and symbolic strategies required by the concept, and (c) data essential to communicating ideas about the concept and for using the concept in decision-making.[11] Also, the input of symbolic materials should be accompanied by provision for memorization of those materials and practice of any strategies involved. This is important when considering the use of symbolic materials. An admonition by Woodruff regarding symbolic materials is that there should be no attempt to introduce new referential input by verbal processes. This would, of course, violate the basic idea of concept formation with its sensory percept intake component.

The final consideration in designing a learning unit is that the unit must provide for any necessary motor learning required for the use of the concept or terminal behavior in adjustment-requiring situations. In other words, if the unit requires an overt behavior, the motor learning to accomplish this behavior must be considered so that the process and goal are consistent.

Studying the basic ideas advanced by Woodruff, it is possible to see some significant implications for teaching and the teacher education process. A discussion of some implications follows.

Implications for Improved Teacher Education

First of all, one might look at Woodruff's work from the point of view of actual activities currently in practice in public school teaching. Woodruff argues that very little effort is being expended in the area of concept formation utilizing sensory input at the first level. There appears to be much more content devoted to the use of verbal symbolic knowledge through books and other writings. This will not adequately foster concept formation if sensory input has not preceded it. This fact is most important for teaching young people, and the ramifications of this idea must be given serious consideration.

Another salient feature of Woodruff's work is that of stating objectives in terms of behaviors and their concepts. The current practice is to draw out the concepts from the content to be taught. According to Woodruff, this is wrong because it gives priority to verbal information instead of to behavior. From the concept, the content necessary to form it adequately must be outlined. In other words, the concept, either process or structural, must be stated and then the content of subject matter, the events and objects of the real world around the student, suggested. Once this is accomplished, the inventory of the student's perceptual intake should be made to determine the level at which the concept formation can begin.

The teacher educator and his students should review carefully these two major ideas and other ideas developed by Woodruff. A basic under-

[11] *Ibid.*

standing of concept formation, the cognitive cycle, and the kinds of concepts identified above is a "must" for the future teacher. Once the understanding is present, then actual experiencing of these ideas is imperative to enable the preservice student to view what is necessary for the concept formation act.

The teacher education student should have a knowledge of and experience in programming experiences for concept formation as advocated by Woodruff. This requires that one understand the concepts, the use of knowledge, and the media and materials appropriate for the unit. Carefully designing the unit according to the principles of concept formation will, therefore, insure a desired outcome.

There are perhaps two other significant implications for teacher educators and students to consider from Woodruff's work. One is the use of media and materials. If the idea of concept formation is to be followed closely, the sensory input area becomes very important. Basic concepts are formed from a direct experience of the real world around the young student. Therefore, the student must perceive these experiences directly from the outside world through various kinds of media and material. Also, if the basic percepts have been previously acquired by the student, the teacher must then move from sensory input to the concept organizing process. This, too, requires media and materials to some extent—to evoke recall, provide focus, and place the percepts in the learning cycle. Thus, media and materials play an important part in concept formation.

The second implication is that the teacher must have a good knowledge of the idea to be taught before he can begin. This requires an understanding of the concepts that the teacher will teach and enough depth on the subject to enable him to show the students, not tell them, to enable the students themselves to build the concepts. Media and materials find their way into this process also.

In summation, to use Woodruff's work on concept formation and designing units for effective teaching may require some significant changes in teacher education. However, if these processes are acquired by the future teacher, a much higher and more analytical level of performance will be practiced in the school classroom. This should be considered a most desirable goal for teacher education.

Bibliography

1. Woodruff, Asahel D. *Basic Concepts of Teaching*. Concise edition. San Francisco: Chandler Publishing Co., 1961.
2. ———. "Characteristics of an Effective Instructional Unit." Working paper prepared for Academic Year Study, State University College, Geneseo, New York, April 14, 1966.
3. ———. "Putting Subject Matter Into Conceptual Form." Paper prepared for TEAM Project meeting, February 6, 1964.
4. ———. "The Nature and Elements of the Cognitive Approach to Instruction." Paper, May 28, 1964 (Mimeo.).
5. ———. *The Psychology of Teaching*. New York: Longmans, Green & Co., 1951.

Chapter 13. Educational Goals

Dean David Krathwohl[1] and his associates have given considerable thought to the area of educational goals, their classification, and the meaning they hold for the educative process. In addition, Krathwohl has considered the place of educational objectives at various levels of detail for the educational process. This chapter will include a review of the role of educational goals at various stages of development of an instructional program and the statements of goals. It will be concluded with implications of goal statements for improving teacher education.

Krathwohl states that educational objectives should be expressed at three levels of specificity, corresponding to three phases of the development of instruction.[2] The first level is the most *general level* and is used primarily for program planning at the broad and abstract level. This involves the statement of goals for types of courses and areas of study for several years of education within a school system. Such a statement of goals at the general level might be developed for the elementary school, the junior high school, or the senior high school. The second level of goal statement is the *intermediate level.* This more concrete level is for curriculum development. This includes behavioral objectives and more specific goals for an instructional course or unit within the curriculum. The third level, the most *specific level,* is geared toward instructional material building and focuses on specific lesson plans and sequencing of specific goals.

To be most useful, statements of goals should be stated in terms of overt behavior that can be seen and measured, because, as Krathwohl argues, specifying educational objectives in terms of behavior is the most meaningful and powerful way to analyze the instructional process. If the teacher holds to the commonly accepted definition that education should

[1] Dr. Krathwohl is Professor of Education and Dean at Syracuse University.

[2] From an all-college address presented at State University College, Geneseo, New York, on April 25, 1966. For a complete discussion on this topic, see Krathwohl (4).

change student behavior, he must state goals in terms of the kinds of behavior desired. The teacher's job is to structure the school situation to enable students to learn appropriate behavior and practice it. Phrasing statements in behavioral terms eliminates poorly defined educational goals.

> Such goals as "the student should become a good citizen" are spelled out in terms of the kinds of behaviors which a good citizen displays. There are then statements, such as, "the student shall be able to identify and appraise judgments and values involved in the choice of a course of political action"; "he shall display skill in identifying different appropriate roles in a democratic group"; or "he will be able to relate principles of civil liberties and civil rights to current events."[3]

With a clear understanding of behavioral objectives the teacher can strive for appropriate behavior from his students. Further, the teacher's task of ascertaining the degree of achievement of goals is much easier, for he needs only to provide appropriate situations which would evoke the desired behavior.

One might argue that if a school system or the teacher makes a statement of goals at the specific level for a given lesson plan, there is no real need for an expression of goals at the two more abstract levels. The specific level is where the actual changing of behavior is occurring. However, Krathwohl suggests that all levels are important for the analysis of the instructional program of the school because:

1. Each level of analysis permits the development of the next more specific level.
2. Mastery objectives can be analyzed to greater specificity than transfer objectives.
3. Curricula gain adoption by consensus that what is taught is of value. Consensus is easily gained at the more abstract levels of analysis.
4. There are usually several alternative ways of analyzing objectives at the more specific level. Objectives at the more abstract level provide a referent for evaluating these alternatives.[4]

In the first instance cited above, there is a need in curriculum building to have a statement of goals moving from the very general and abstract to the very specific behaviors desired in the classroom. In the example on citizenship cited above, one can see the need for a general expression of goals at the abstract level, followed by a more specific expression of behaviors. Each level of expression guides the total development of the one following.

In his second statement, Krathwohl suggests that not all goals can be completely specified at the third level. Some objectives—for instance, the recall of the sums of pairs of numbers below ten—can be specified in complete detail; and all the possible examples of the behavior can be specified, i.e., the possible pairs of numbers between zero and nine. Other objectives can be specified only at the general level, since specific applications cannot

---

[3] Krathwohl (4), p. 84.

[4] *Ibid.*, p. 86.

be anticipated. Further, one cannot specify various modifications in behavior needed in the variety of situations in which it will be used. Consider as examples the appreciation of use of shading and color in painting or the ability to effectively address an audience.

In his third argument, Krathwohl suggests that consensus of educational goals is more possible at the very abstract levels. Few educators would argue with the general level goal that a student should become a good citizen, but agreement might be difficult to reach concerning how to effect specific behavior leading to this general goal. In this case the general objective is a point from which the more specific goals can be defined. The general goal can be changed when necessary, as can the specific goals.

Finally, Krathwohl suggests that there are several ways to move from the intermediate to the very specific level. The analysis of specifics becomes much easier, because the intermediate level provides selected referents for evaluating the specific alternatives. This is important for the educative process, because it promotes analytic behavior by the classroom teacher.

The Use of Taxonomies

It appears quite clear that there must be a statement of objectives at three levels to increase analyses of educational goals in behavioral terms. Krathwohl focuses attention on measures to facilitate the statements of objectives.

For the intermediate level Krathwohl suggests that the taxonomies[5] have been quite useful in analyzing objectives. The two taxonomies will therefore receive some attention here.

The taxonomies grew out of a desire to eliminate confusion regarding evaluation of educational objectives. These writings attempted to develop some commonality in terms used between evaluators and between institutions. With a common, precise means of communicating educational goals, some sharing of learning devices, materials, and curricula could occur. The taxonomy used by Krathwohl is basically a classification system of the kinds of behavior that should result from a learning session; therefore, pupil behavior is emphasized. Each behavioral objective is divided into two parts: the behavior the student should demonstrate and the subject matter or content used by the student. Behaviorally-stated teacher goals are Krathwohl's main concern; the taxonomy does not classify the content or subject matter itself.

Two taxonomies have been developed and published: the cognitive domain and the affective domain. There is an investigation to determine the feasibility of developing the Psycho-Motor Domain, which would include physical education and technical subjects.

Krathwohl describes the taxonomies as follows:

> Basically the taxonomy is an educational-logical-psychological classification system. The terms in this order reflect the emphasis given to the organizing

[5] See Bloom, *et al.* (1), and Krathwohl, *et al.* (2).

principles upon which it is built. It makes educational distinctions in the sense that the boundaries between categories reflect the decisions that teachers make among student behaviors in their development of curriculum, and in choosing learning situations. It is a logical system in the sense that its terms are defined precisely and are used consistently. In addition, each category permits logical subdivisions which can be clearly defined and further subdivided as necessary and useful. Finally the taxonomy seems to be consistent with our present understanding of psychological phenomena, though it does not rest on any single theory.

The scheme is intended to be purely descriptive so that every type of educational goal can be represented. It does not indicate the value or quality of one class as compared to another. It is impartial with respect to views of education. One of the tests of the taxonomy has been that of inclusiveness—could [it] only classify all kinds of educational objectives (if stated as student behaviors) in the framework? In general, it seems to have met this test.[6]

Cognitive Domain

The cognitive domain is basically divided into a category labeled "knowledge" and five categories of the skills and abilities to use this knowledge. A brief outline of the cognitive domain follows:

1.00 *Knowledge*

- 1.10 *Knowledge of Specifics*
  - 1.11 *Knowledge of Terminology*
  - 1.12 *Knowledge of Specific Facts*
- 1.20 *Knowledge of Ways and Means of Dealing With Specifics*
  - 1.21 *Knowledge of Conventions*
  - 1.22 *Knowledge of Trends and Sequences*
  - 1.23 *Knowledge of Classifications and Categories*
  - 1.24 *Knowledge of Criteria*
  - 1.25 *Knowledge of Methodology*
- 1.30 *Knowledge of the Universals and Abstractions in a Field*
  - 1.31 *Knowledge of Principles and Generalizations*
  - 1.32 *Knowledge of Theories and Structures*

2.00 *Comprehension*

- 2.10 *Translation*
- 2.20 *Interpretation*
- 2.30 *Extrapolation*

3.00 *Application*

4.00 *Analysis*

- 4.10 *Analysis of Elements*
- 4.20 *Analysis of Relationships*
- 4.30 *Analysis of Organizational Principles*

---

[6] Krathwohl (3), p. 21.

5.00 *Synthesis*

5.10 *Production of a Unique Communication*

5.20 *Production of a Plan, or Proposed Set of Operations*

5.30 *Derivation of a Set of Abstract Relations*

6.00 *Evaluation*

6.10 *Judgments in Terms of Internal Evidence*

6.20 *Judgments in Terms of External Criteria*[7]

Within the taxonomy on the cognitive domain, there are subcategories, definitions, illustrative objectives taken from educational literature, a summary of the kinds of test items that can be used in each category, some discussion on the problems involved in evaluating behavior in each category, and many examples of test items.

Krathwohl states that this *Taxonomy* is hierarchical in nature, because each category is included within the next higher category. Each category requires the behavior of the one previous to it, thus effecting a simple to complex motion. He further states:

> Perhaps the idea of the continuum is most easily gained from looking at the major headings of the cognitive domain, which include knowledge (recall of facts, principles, etc.), comprehension (ability to restate knowledge in new words), application (understanding well enough to break it apart into its parts and make the relations among ideas explicit), synthesis (the ability to produce wholes from parts, to produce a plan of operation, to derive a set of abstract relations), and evaluation (the ability to judge the value of material for given purposes.[8]

Affective Domain

Krathwohl states that there are poorer educational objectives in the affective domain than in the cognitive domain. Many problems exist in defining appreciation, value, and attitude. In developing the taxonomy, an attempt was made to attach certain meanings to terms such as interest, value, attitudes, and appreciations. This was abandoned in favor of the use of a process called "internalization" as a structuring principle for the hierarchical framework of the *Taxonomy*. Internalization in this case means the change or inner growth that occurs in an individual as he becomes aware of and adopts certain attitudes and principles which are inherent in forming selected value judgments and behaving according to his values. Krathwohl suggests that it is quite similar to socialization. An understanding of the internalization process may be gained from a study of the taxonomy structure of the affective domain, discussed below and shown in outline form in this chapter.

> We begin with the individual's being aware of the stimuli which initiate the affective behavior and which form the context in which the affective behavior occurs. Thus, the lowest category is 1.0 *Receiving*. It is subdivided into

[7] Bloom, *et al.* (1).

[8] Krathwohl (4), p. 87.

three categories. At the 1.1 *Awareness* level, the individual merely has his attention attracted to the stimuli (e.g., he develops some consciousness of the use of shading to portray depth and lighting in a picture). The second subcategory, 1.2 *Willingness to Receive,* describes the state in which he has differentiated the stimuli from others and is willing to give his attention (e.g., he develops a tolerance for bizarre uses of shading in modern art). At 1.3 *Controlled or Selected Attention,* the student looks for the stimuli (e.g., he is on the alert for instances where shading has been used both to create a sense of three-dimensional depth and to indicate the lighting of the picture; or he looks for picturesque words in reading).

At the next level, 2.0 *Responding,* the individual is perceived as responding regularly to the affective stimuli. At the lowest level of responding, 2.1 *Acquiescence in Responding,* he is merely complying with expectations (e.g., at the request of his teacher, he hangs reproductions of famous paintings in his dormitory room; he is obedient to traffic rules). At the next higher level, 2.2 *Willingness to Respond,* he responds increasingly to an inner compulsion (e.g., voluntarily looks for instances of good art where shading, perspective, color, and design have been well used, or has an interest in social problems broader than those of the local community). At 2.3 *Satisfaction in Response,* he responds emotionally as well (e.g., works with clay, especially in making pottery for personal pleasure). Up to this point he has differentiated the affective stimuli; he has begun to seek them out and to attach emotional significance and value to them.

As the process unfolds, the next levels of 3.0 *Valuing* describe increasing internalization, as the person's behavior is sufficiently consistent that he comes to hold a value: 3.1 *Acceptance of a Value* (e.g., continuing desire to develop the ability to write effectively and hold it more strongly); 3.2 *Preference for a Value* (e.g., seeks out examples of good art for enjoyment of them to the level where he behaves so as to further this impression actively); and 3.3 *Commitment* (e.g., faith in the power of reason and the method of experimentation).

As the learner successively internalizes values, he encounters situations for which more than one value is relevant. This necessitates organizing the values into a system, 4.0 *Organization.* And since a prerequisite to interrelating values is their conceptualization in a form which permits organization, this level is divided in two 4.1 *Conceptualization of a Value* (e.g., desires to evaluate works of art which are appreciated, or to find out and crystallize the basic assumptions which underlie codes of ethics) and 4.2 *Organization of a Value System* (e.g., acceptance of the place of art in one's life as one of dominant value, or weighs alternative social policies and practices against the standards of public welfare).

Finally, the internalization and the organization processes reach a point where the individual responds very consistently to value-laden situations with an interrelated set of values, a structure, a view of the world. The taxonomy category that describes this behavior is 5.0 *Characterization by a Value or Value Complex;* and it includes the categories 5.1 *Generalized Set* (e.g., views all problems in terms of their aesthetic aspects, or readiness to revise judgments and to change behavior in the light of evidence) and 5.2 *Characterization* (e.g., develops a consistent philosophy of life).

Stripped of their definitions, the category and subcategory titles appear in sequence as follows:

1.00 *Receiving (Attending)*

- 1.10 *Awareness*
- 1.20 *Willingness to Receive*
- 1.30 *Controlled or Selected Attention*

2.00 *Responding*

2.10 *Acquiescence in Responding*
2.20 *Willingness to Respond*
2.30 *Satisfaction in Response*

3.00 *Valuing*

3.10 *Acceptance of a Value*
3.20 *Preference for a Value*
3.30 *Commitment*

4.00 *Organization*

4.10 *Conceptualization*
4.20 *Organization of a Value System*

5.00 *Characterization by a Value or Value Complex*

5.10 *Generalized Set*
5.20 *Characterization*[9]

Within the intermediate level of educational goals, the taxonomies appear, then, to provide sufficient assistance and potential usefulness for working out measures of stating and evaluating appropriate objectives. At the instructional material building level, Krathwohl suggests that Robert Gagné has made some significant inroads for specifying objectives. Gagné has suggested some categories which blend behavioristic psychology and cognitive theory, and which are hierarchical, because one capability or behavior depends in a large part upon the learning of some other simpler one. Gagné's categories in outline form are:

1. Strategies
   and
2. Problem Solving
   which require the pre-learning of:
3. Principles
   which require the pre-learning of:
4. Concepts
   which require the pre-learning of:
5. Associations
   which require the pre-learning of:
6. Chains
   which require the pre-learning of:
7. Identifications
   which require the pre-learning of:
8. Responses.[10]

Gagné further suggests that the categories of problem-solving and the development of strategies are the highest forms which tie together the

---

[9] Krathwohl, *et al.* (2), pp. 34-35.

[10] Gagné (5).

principles developed at the third level. In this hierarchical category system, the upper four deal with cognitive theory and the lower four with behavioristic psychology. The potential of this category system should be recalled when considering the instructional material building level defined by Krathwohl.[11]

Krathwohl sees real potential for the statement of goals utilizing some of the categories mentioned above. The taxonomies have real meaning for curriculum building because of their hierarchical nature. Both the affective and cognitive domains can assist curriculum builders to achieve a high degree of consistency at the intermediate level of goal statement specificity, within a school, school system, or series of schools. Using the taxonomies as guides can foster an interchange of experiences between schools and can encourage comparisons of curriculum patterns. This indeed makes the taxonomies very useful tools for stating and analyzing curriculum objectives.

A final word of admonition advanced by Krathwohl is that objectives within the affective domain have been under-emphasized recently in comparison to the cognitive domain. Thus, objectives have been primarily considered in only one domain. He further suggests that most cognitive domain statements reflect to some degree an interest in the affective. The development of "interest" in a particular subject matter area, often expressed by teachers, reflects concern for the affective domain. In such cases a separate goal statement should be developed to stress affective goals. Every teacher assessing changes in his students' behavior should be aware of this important concern. The erosion of affective goals, from the point of stating objectives to their evaluation, should receive serious attention from teachers and curriculum workers. Even though assessing affective changes over a short length of time (e.g., one year) is difficult, this assessment is most important for schools in a democratic society.

Implications for Improved Teacher Education

Utilization of the taxonomy, as well as other systems, is meaningful to the educative process in terms of the power of educational objectives stated behaviorally. The process may force the educator to a level of specificity concerning what is being done in the classroom. When one thinks about behavioral objectives and the use of the taxonomies, he becomes more specific in his goal statement, his methodology, and his evaluation. Further, he begins to develop a language with specific definitions which provides a vehicle for communication on curriculum design, sequencing, integration of experiences, etc., in a manner which transcends individual grades and teachers. The implications for curriculum building and innovation are great, and the development of more analytic behavior in the educator is very possible.

---

[11] See also Gagné, Robert M. *Conditions of Learning.* New York: Holt, Rinehart & Winston, 1965.

The teacher educator and his students should give particular attention to these important features of using the taxonomy and other frameworks. Developing ideas of the early use of the taxonomy for curriculum building, for designating specific behavioral outcomes, and for encouraging appropriate communication techniques seems to be most important for the future teacher. Krathwohl suggests that the development of a more analytic behavior concerning educational objectives should come early in the student's preservice training, and most important of all, the study and use of the taxonomies should continue in a spiral fashion throughout the entire preparatory program. In other words, the student's awareness of behavioral goals and of behavioral outcomes must be ever present in his preservice work. In this case, then, the student should return continuously to the taxonomies to make his work meaningful and to acquire the analytic behavior necessary for effective teaching. Also, this awareness of specifying and accomplishing behavioral goals may increase the use of affective objectives, which appears to be important.

Krathwohl suggests that the early exposure to and understanding of educational objectives can be accomplished at the experience level through the analysis of examinations, lesson plans, teacher tasks, and standardized tests. Once the significance of behavioral goals is understood, the student can begin to use them in his teaching situations. At this point, the development of the analytic behavior for specifying and using behavioral objectives begins. A behavioral goal such as this on the part of a future teacher is one with which few teacher educators would argue.

Bibliography

1. Bloom, Benjamin S. and others. *Taxonomy of Educational Objectives, The Classification of Educational Goals, Handbook I: Cognitive Domain.* New York: David McKay, 1956.
2. Krathwohl, David R., Bloom, Benjamin S., and Masia, B. *Taxonomy of Educational Objectives, The Classification of Educational Goals, Handbook II: Affective Domain.* New York: David McKay, 1964.
3. ———. "The Taxonomy of Educational Objectives and its Use in Curriculum Building." *Defining Educational Objectives.* Edited by C. M. Lindvall. Pittsburgh: University of Pittsburgh Press, 1964. Chapter 3, pp. 19-36.
4. ———. "Stating Objectives Appropriately for Program, for Curriculum, and for Instructional Materials Development." *Journal of Teacher Education* 16: 83-92; March 1965.
5. ———. Gagné, Robert M. "The Implications of Instructional Objectives for Learning." *Defining Educational Objectives.* Edited by C. M. Lindvall. Pittsburgh: University of Pittsburgh Press, 1964.

Chapter 14. Theories of Instruction

Professor Elizabeth Steiner Maccia[1] has devoted considerable time and effort to educational theorizing. This chapter will be based on her notions on theories, scientific theory development and formal instruction, and her descriptive theory of instruction. Some implications of her work for improved teacher education will conclude this chapter.

To begin with, Maccia suggests that educational theorizing is important, for education is no longer based on mere speculating. There seems to be, in fact, a crucial need for theoretical work, particularly in the area of research. It is within this realm that Maccia has suggested her claims for a theory and the appropriate verification of these claims.

Maccia views a theory as a related and systematic set of statements. The relatedness and coherence of statements, or actually propositions, are the important criteria for any kind of theory. She states:

> Theories may be either formal or descriptive or prescriptive. The statements of a formal theory—theories of pure logic and pure mathematics—are given no meaning; they are not interpreted. The statements of a descriptive theory—theories of empirical science—are given meaning through what is; they are interpreted experientially. The statements of prescriptive theory—theories of philosophy—are given meaning through what ought to be; they are interpreted ideally.[2]

Maccia suggests that the three important kinds of educational theorizing are as follows:

> 1. theorizing about educational reality which I shall call "event educational theorizing,"
> 2. theorizing about behavioral outcomes of education which I shall call "valuational educational theorizing," and

---

[1] Dr. Maccia, formerly Professor of Philosophy of Education, and co-director of the Educational Theory Center and the Social Studies Curriculum Center of The Ohio State University, is Professor of Philosophy at the University of Southwestern Louisiana where she will develop both an undergraduate and a graduate program in philosophy.

[2] Maccia (3), p. 88.

3. theorizing about the logic or structure of languages in education which I shall call "formal educational theorizing."

One is a scientific enterprise, while two and three are philosophical ones.[3]

Maccia further suggests that even some theorizing about practices is necessary. This fourth kind of theorizing can be termed "praxiological." In discussing this she states:

> . . . it is a scientific enterprise. It is not the case, however, that this fourth kind of educational theorizing can be reduced simply to a combination of the other three. To be sure, praxiological educational theorizing depends upon the other three kinds: valuational educational theorizing offers possible behavioral outcomes for which means could be developed and to which so related, and event educational theorizing and formal educational theorizing indicate the interrelations required in the practices. Nevertheless, involved in praxiological educational theorizing is the development of new events (specially constructed teacher actions, student actions, and material objects) which are combined into practices.[4]

Figure I summarizes the total task of educational theorizing.

Figure I.—Kinds of Education Theorizing.[5]

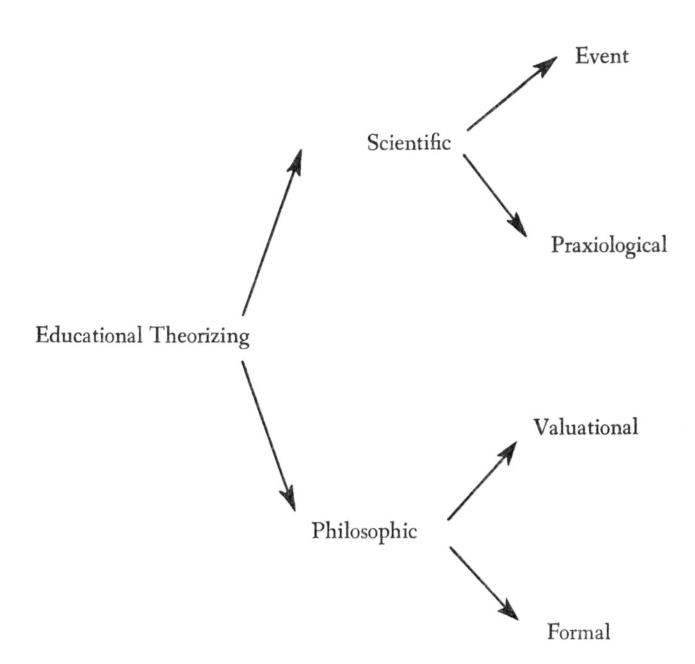

[3] Maccia (1), p. 4.

[4] *Ibid.*, pp. 4-5.

[5] *Ibid.*, p. 5.

Educational theorizing as seen from a scientific inquiry point of view will be closely examined. This now seems important to educational research and investigation. Maccia suggests that the complete act of inquiry has two important dimensions: the development of cognitive claims and the justification of the claims. The construction and the checking of cognitive claims must, then, receive attention. Maccia outlines the complete act of scientific inquiry as follows:

Figure II.—The Complete Act of Scientific Inquiry.[6]

1. Development of Cognitive Claims: Theory Construction Tasks
   - 1.1. Setting forth Terms (Variables)
   - 1.2. Relating Terms (Variables) to Form Propositions (Hypotheses)
   - 1.3. Relating Propositions (Hypotheses) to Form Theory

2. Justification of Cognitive Claims: Theory Verification Tasks
   - 2.1. Collection of Data
     - 2.1.1. Specification of Indicators
     - 2.1.2. Specification of Design
   - 2.2. Interpretation of Data

In discussing the tasks in Figure II, Maccia suggests:

> If an inquiry is scientific, it includes development of a hypothesis or hypotheses about reality. A hypothesis is a not-yet-checked claim about relations between aspects of reality, and these relations are asserted to extend beyond a given time and given place. A hypothesis takes the form of a generalized proposition, a statemental assertion of a relation between classes (variables). A hypothesis or hypotheses must be in the context of other hypotheses. A single unrelated hypothesis or a heap of unrelated hypotheses offers no cognitive claim. Knowledge is adequate theory, and theory is a set of related hypotheses. It is patent, consequently, that the development of cognitive claims in science is theory construction.
>
> If an inquiry is scientific, it also includes justification by means of observations of instances falling under the hypothesis that the variable can be observed in the instances. For example, an indicator of reading readiness is a portion of the *Metropolitan Readiness Tests*. Furthermore, the arrangement to produce the readings of indicators (a design for data) must be set forth. Solomon Four Group Design is, of course, an illustration of an arrangement which is experimental in nature. Different designs give different plausibilities with respect to hypotheses. This plausibility enters into the interpretation of the data. Ascertainment of the generality possible from the instances checked is of primary importance here. Clearly, justification of cognitive claims in science is theory verification.[7]

---

[6] Maccia (4), p. 5.

[7] Maccia (4), p. 3.

Figure II in essence indicates the complete act of scientific inquiry and also the relationship between researching and theorizing. In separating the two tasks, it must be kept in mind that one task depends on the other. Theory has little meaning if verification is not possible, and verification procedures must be adjusted to the theory. The theory construction task should be modified if verification does not exist. Once there is some consistency between the two areas, the theoretical system can be utilized.

In the development of theory construction tasks, Maccia utilizes her Theory Models approach. In this case, the model serves as a starting point for theory development. She states:

> A model is an object or a characterization used either to represent or to be represented. When an object or characterization is used to represent, it is a model of; when used to be represented, a model for. A model of is called a *representational model;* and a model for *a non-representational model.* In scientific inquiry, the characterizations of interest are generalized propositions which set forth relations between aspects of reality. The characterizations, thus, are empirical in nature. All propositions, whether they be empirical or not, have form. That is to say, the proposition is structured in a certain way (the terms are interrelated in a certain way) and the group of propositions is structured in a certain way (the propositions are interrelated in a certain way). The characterizations, thus, are also formal in nature. The content can be taken from an empirical characterization, and the remainder would be a formal characterization.[8]

Figure III summarizes and illustrates the kinds of models discernable in a scientific context. The illustrations are given in terms of language behavior, of which reading is a part.

Figure III.—Kinds of Models and Illustrations.[9]

1. Representational

   1.1. Object : a programmed computer used to represent an aspect of language behavior, i.e. simulation of actual language behavior through a programmed computer

   1.2. Characterization

      1.2.1. Empirical : a proposition about language behavior used to represent the actual language behavior, i.e. theory of language behavior

      1.2.2. Formal : the formal component of the propositions (the way in which the terms and propositions are interrelated) used to represent the actual interrelations of aspects of language behavior and related events, i.e. the formal component of theory of language behavior.

[8] Maccia (4), pp. 4 and 6.

[9] *Ibid.*, p. 7.

Figure III, continued

2. Non-representational		
2.1. Object	:	a programmed computer used to be represented in language behavior
2.2. Characterization		
2.2.1. Empirical	:	propositions characterizing messages when they are taken to be outputs of a Markov process used to be represented in a theory of language behavior
2.2.2. Formal	:	Markov process used to be represented in a theory of language behavior

She continues by stating that, "Not all kinds of models discernable in a scientific context are of significance for scientific theorizing. Some kinds may be of no significance for scientific inquiry, and some kinds may be of significance for scientific inquiry, and some kinds may be of significance only for scientific verification."[10] Figure IV (p. 129) indicates the significance of the various kinds of models for scientific inquiry.

In discussing Figure IV, Maccia states:

> Non-representational objects are of no significance for scientific inquiry, but representational objects are. It is through objects formed to represent instances that theory which could not be verified becomes susceptible of verification. The difficulty of unavailable instances is overcome by simulation. Also of significance for verification procedures are representational characterizations. Models of data, e.g. Gaussian distribution, are essential in collection and interpretation of data. Representational characterizations are of no significance for theorizing. In theorizing, characterizations must be developed. What is needed are characterizations from which to devise characterizations. Models for (non-representational models) are required.[11]

The conclusion that non-representational models of the characterization kind are significant for scientific inquiry led to Maccia's formulation of her Theory Models approach. In this case, Maccia suggests that theorizing cannot be done inductively. Theory is necessary to make sense out of data just as data is necessary to verify theory. Percepts without concepts are blind, and concepts without percepts are empty. Thus, in scientific inquiry, theorizing must take place before researching.

Maccia's approach to theorizing is not reductive, where one theory in a particular field is used for a theory in another. It is also not deductive, where one searches for a theory in another discipline from which the

[10] *Ibid.*, p. 6.

[11] *Ibid.*, pp. 6 and 9.

Figure IV.—Kinds of Models and Their Significance for Scientific Inquiry.[12]

Model			Theorizing	Verifying
Representational	Object		0	1
Representational	Characterization	Empirical	0	1
Representational	Characterization	Formal	0	1
Non-representational	Object		0	0
Non-representational	Characterization	Empirical	1	0
Non-representational	Characterization	Formal	1	0

'1' denotes significance

'0' denotes no significance

[12] *Ibid.*, p. 8.

wanted theory in one's discipline can be deduced. These approaches may be represented as follows:

Figure V.—Reductive and Deductive Approach.[13]

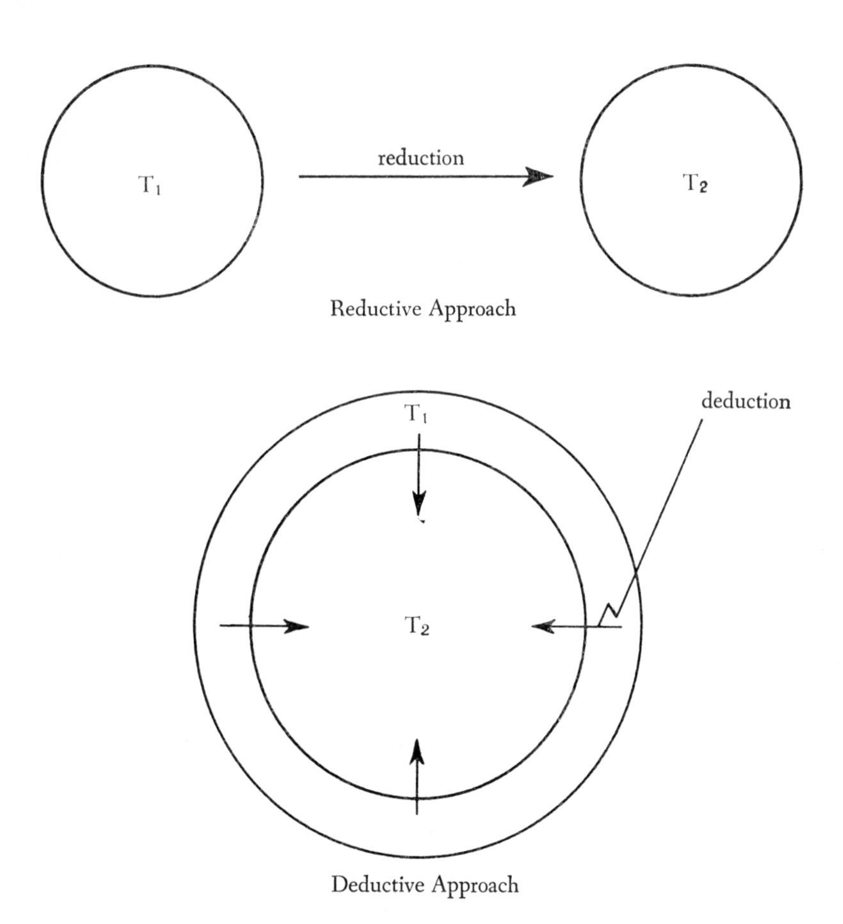

'T_1' denotes theory from which T_2, the wanted theory, is to be obtained. 'T_M' denotes the theory model. T_1 and T_2, of course, are equivalent only in the reductive approach.

Rather the theory models approach is retroductive. In this case theory is not taken for theory, but theory is taken as a model of theory. She states:

> In forming the theory model, elements from the theory are selected and arranged. The elements may be modified in any way required for a point-of-

[13] *Ibid.*, p. 13.

view which will lead to the devising of adequate theory. From the theory model, one devises the theory. It is important to note that there is no *a priori way* of determining whether a theory model will produce an adequate theory just as there is no *a priori way* of determining whether a theory is adequate. The theory model must be tried out. Stated differently, just as theorizing should be done in a context of data, so theory model forming should be in the context of theorizing. This process of devising is called retroductive, since the theory that is devised (conclusion) contains more than the theory from which it was devised (premises). The implication, therefore, can only lead back from conclusion to premises.[14]

Figure VI summarizes the Theory Models approach to educational theorizing.

Figure VI.—Theory Models Approach.[15]

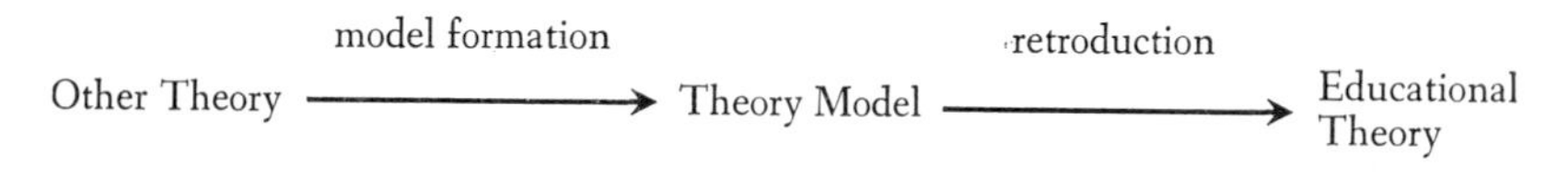

(or)

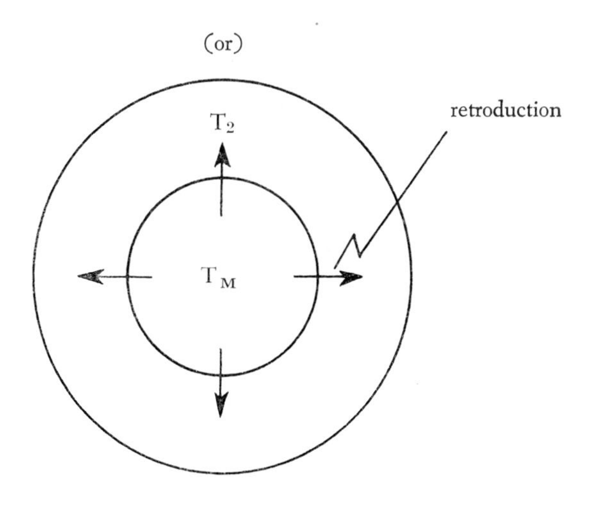

Retroductive (Theory Models) Approach

Finally, the Theory Models approach might appear to be redundant, because a theory is taken to be a model insofar as a theory represents some aspect of reality. However, Maccia states that "identification of theory and model which is rooted in the representational sense of 'model' leads to a disregard of the approach to theory construction in which one theory is a model for yet another theory, but is not the same as the theory for which it is a model. Unless models are considered as a source of theory, they cannot function in theory construction."[16]

---

[14] *Ibid.*, pp. 11-12.

[15] *Ibid.*, pp. 12-13.

[16] *Ibid.*, p. 12.

Using her theory construction ideas, Maccia moves to a discussion of her theory of formal instruction. She confines her theory to formal instruction within the context of the school. To include all of life as instruction (e.g., home or church) would not permit a sufficiently limited domain for delineating a distinctive area of educational inquiry. Thus she sees the term "formal instruction" as the interaction of interrelationships of teaching and learning within the school. This can be represented diagrammatically as follows:

Figure VII.—Formal Instruction Within the School.[17]

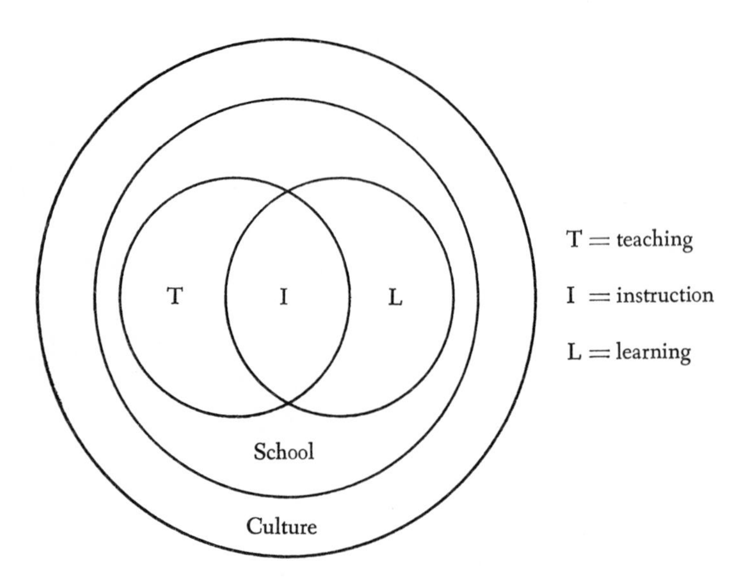

Within the realm of a theory on formal instruction, Maccia again states that any scientific theory, to be adequate, must display formal coherence, observational verification, and observational predictiveness.

> The meaning of this discussion of adequacy criteria can be resolved into questions to ask as the theory is presented. With respect to formal coherence, ask these questions:
>
> 1. Do the ideas about instruction fit together?
>
> 2. If the ideas about instruction do not fit together, could they be extended or modified or both in order to produce the fit?
>
> 3. Do the ideas about instruction check with experimental or non-experimental observations recorded by others or made by you?
>
> 4. If there is no evidence as to whether the ideas about instruction check with observations, could experimental or non-experimental designs for checking them be devised?

---

[17] Maccia, in seminar discussion.

With respect to observational predictiveness, ask this question:

5. From ideas about instruction, could other ideas about instruction be derived (hypotheses be stated), and could these predictions be observed (experimental or non-experimental designs for checking the hypotheses be devised)?[18]

Maccia sees instruction within the relationship of teaching and learning *as an influence toward rule-governed behavior.* Thus the factors of group dynamics and the discipline approach to curriculum appear important. A brief discussion of each will focus attention on their meaning for a theory of instruction.

Maccia views group dynamics as an inquiry to advance knowledge of group life, not as role playing or a political ideology. This is consistent with scientific theorizing since the concern is located with structure variables that are descriptive of internal behavior of the group and consist of statements of relations among group members.

The interpersonal relations in a classroom can be identified clearly in two positions: the teacher and the student. Maccia identifies the teacher as the inducer of behavioral change; the student is the inducee. Thus it is that teaching, inducing behavioral change, is differentiated from learning and is the directed relation of the two positions. The directed relation can be seen diagrammatically through graph theory as follows:

Figure VIII.

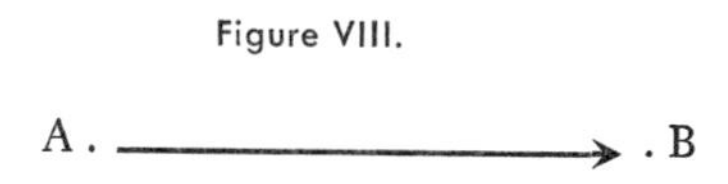

This direct relation points to a concept of influence, A influences B, and thus will be called "an influence relation."

Influence relations could be direct or indirect. Figure VIII shows a direct influence relation, while Figure IX shows a direct influence relation of A over B and of B over C, and an indirect one of A over C.

Figure IX.

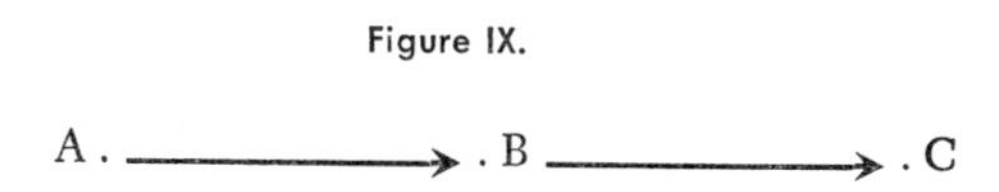

Furthermore, there could be mutual influence, where each person is both teacher and student, as in Figure X.

Figure X.

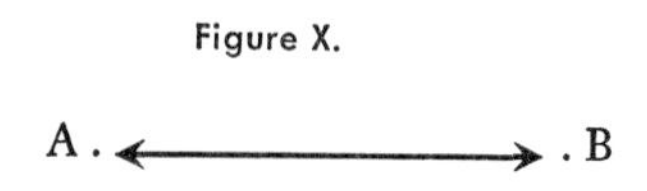

It must be obvious from the foregoing statements that there are many possibilities as to the influence structure of a given classroom. It is not the

[18] Maccia (3), pp. 89-90.

case that a classroom group necessarily has the influence structure of Figure XI because A is hired as the teacher and B, C, and D are enrolled as students.

Figure XI.

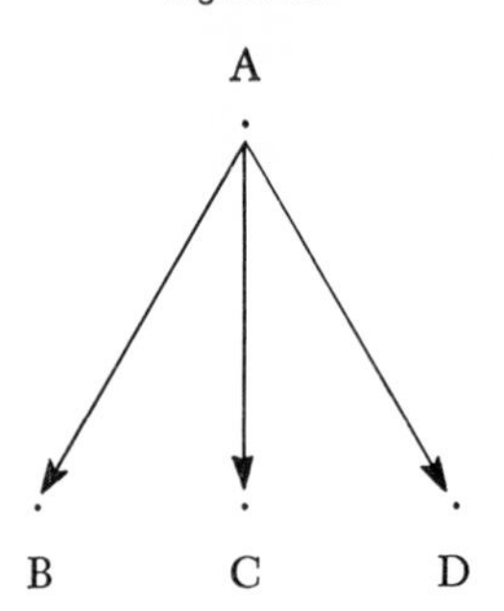

The classroom group might be structured according to Figures XII, XIII, XIV, or XV.

In Figure XII, A directly teaches B and indirectly C, through B directly teaching C. D is isolate, and taught by no one. In Figure XIII, the hired teacher, A, teaches no one. Student C teaches B and D; and C is actually not a student, since he is taught by no one. In Figure XIV, there are two teachers, A and C, who both directly teach B and D, the two students. What if A's and C's teachings are contradictory? In Figure XV, every person is both teacher and student.

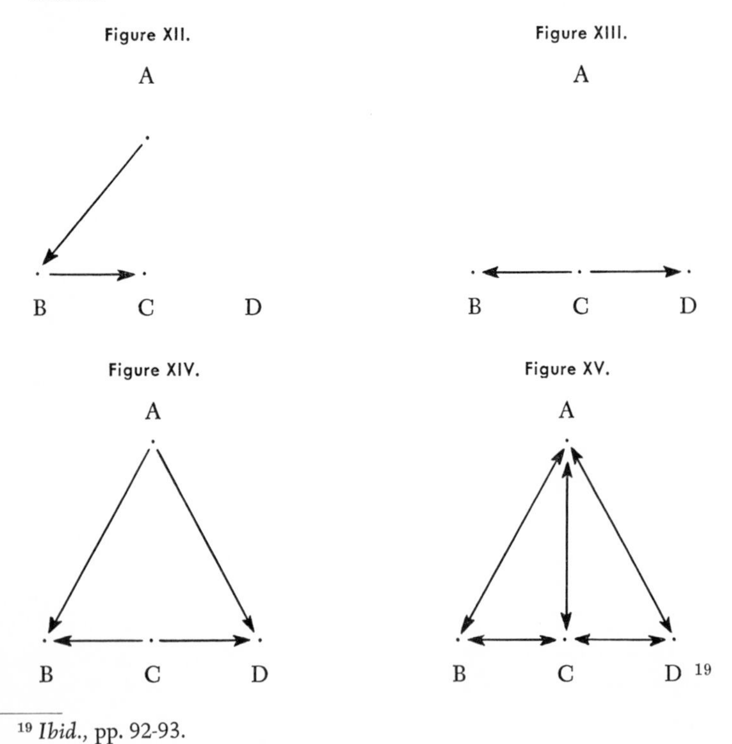

[19]

[19] *Ibid.*, pp. 92-93.

Some decision must be made now as to what kind of influence structure is desirable in the classroom. This decision, Maccia suggests, is a matter of philosophical theorizing, not scientific theorizing, and involves some degree of motivation in the one being influenced.

In her analysis of motivational factors, Maccia suggests that things such as punishment, reward, legitimacy, expertise, and affect can provide influence in the classroom. Reward and punitive measures are obvious, while legitimacy of position is a consequence of being hired as a teacher. The teacher's expertise is independent of the group's valuing, and it influences the students because the group judges the teacher as he ought to be. Affection for an individual can be a source of influence resulting from a positive feeling toward the individual. Maccia suggests that limited work has been done in this area of influence, and only after more effort can one determine how influence is involved in the teaching-learning process.

Within the second dimension of Maccia's theory of instruction, the discipline approach to curriculum, she suggests that discipline could mean: (a) instruction or teaching, or (b) regulation or control. In the latter case, instruction means learning or behavioral change as regulated or controlled behavior, behavior governed by rules. Maccia defines a rule as "a reason or criterion which leads to one behavior rather than another behavior. It is a way of behaving rather than another way. It is judgment or selective in nature. The selective characteristic of a rule also makes it a way of solving problems, since problems are sets of alternatives. In an individual, a rule is a cognitive structure. Through teaching, cognitive structures are built up in a student, or to state the matter in another way, the student becomes a problem-solver."[20]

Maccia suggests that discipline could be defined in other ways which suggest more control and also hinder theorizing. Discipline in addition could mean: (c) control through punishment, and (d) submission to authority. The four meanings involve the motivational bases suggested above, because one involves punitive measures and the other includes all five kinds of motivation. These factors limit cognition since they hinder a person's actions. Maccia suggests that the individual is a problem-solver and that human behavior must be described in these terms. The student is thus active and not passive, and desires to relate to the content presented by the teacher. The student can relate in this manner only if he has appropriate cognitive structures and behavioral rules.

Finally Maccia suggests two other meanings of discipline: (e) organized branches of knowledge, and (f) rules of practical conduct, both of which can be utilized for her theory of rule-governed behavior. It may appear that these two meanings are mutually exclusive, but Maccia argues that practical conduct can occur within the bounds of a discipline. Businessmen, doctors, and carpenters have their ways of problem solving com-

[20] *Ibid.*, p. 96.

parable to those of academicians. Rules for problem solving are not restricted to the ways of science, literature, and other disciplines. Basic structuring of the disciplines, as in science, is necessary before problem solving can occur.

In summation, for instruction in schools, Maccia suggests that:

> What is required is simply the introduction into the content of instruction (the curriculum) problems covering all aspects of human living. But the introduction of problems demands knowledge of structure. To introduce a problem of a given aspect of human living is to introduce at the same time the way of solving the problem. A problem to be a problem must have some structure or organization. A problem is present only if there is doubt or uncertainty. Doubt or uncertainty is present if alternatives are present and so require selection. To select is to solve a problem. If content is completely unstructured or disorganized, alternatives cannot be discerned and no selection is possible. If content is completely structured or organized, there are no alternatives and no selection is required. Total uncertainty or certainty is nonproblematic. A problem, therefore, to be a problem of a given aspect of human living must have some structuring or organizing along the lines of the organization of that aspect of human living. The problem must incorporate rules or cognitive structures or ways of solving problems distinctive to that kind of human living.
>
> The discipline approach to the curriculum has led to learning as rule-governed behavior or problem solving. The possible learnings, and so the possible instructional content (curriculum), have not been restricted within narrow bounds. All possibilities of human living could be matters of learning. The "could" looms large, since actualization of possibilities awaits analysis of the structure of realms of rule-governed behavior other than science. Such analysis would provide the teacher the necessary knowledge to be the kind of problem-maker who could offer instructional content which, if also appropriate, could lead to rule-governed behavior for all aspects of human living. Whether the teacher ought to offer all or only some instructional content would be a matter of prescriptive theorizing. I would assume most of our prescriptive theorizing would agree in placing the thieving aspects of human living outside of instructional bounds.[21]

From the review of Maccia's notions on theory, theory building, and the theory of formal instruction, one can begin to glean some implications for the improvement of the teacher education process. A discussion of implications follows.

Implications for Improved Teacher Education

Maccia herself suggests that the teacher educator and his students should have some working knowledge of what an educational theory is composed, how it can be constructed, and how it can be tested and verified. She feels that the entire teacher education professional component should be inquiry-oriented, whereby the students and instructor explore together the study of education. Having a sophisticated knowledge base of theory and theory development provides the students with the tools to do this, and removes to a certain degree the old trial-and-error way of operating.

---

[21] *Ibid.*, pp. 98-99.

This knowledge base adds to the analytic behavior of the young student who will in time assume his position in a school.

The exploration of theories and theory construction can be accomplished by the instructor who keeps the work at the level of the students. Perceiving these sophisticated notions at the student's level of understanding will lead to more meaning and move the student to the stage of becoming inquiry-oriented. This type of instruction requires instructor awarness of Maccia's basic notions.

Maccia emphasizes what appear to be two salient ideas for her theory of formal instruction: (a) solving problems covering all aspects of human living, (b) having a knowledge of the structure in content organization. These important ideas must receive careful attention from the teacher educator and his students. Effective problem solving can occur only when doubt or uncertainty is present, which can occur only when alternatives are present for selection. Only the correct organization and structure of the content can lead to appropriate alternatives for selecting and testing. These are the prerequisites for solving human problems. The future teacher must have both experience in significant problem solving and also a good knowledge of the content area. This is no simple task; but if it can produce a sophisticated, analytical teacher for the classroom, it is well worth the effort.

Bibliography

1. Maccia, Elizabeth Steiner. *Educational Theorizing and Curriculum Change.* Columbus, Ohio: Bureau of Educational Research and Service, The Ohio State University, 1966.

2. ———, Maccia, George S. and Jewett, Robert E. *Construction of Educational Theory Models.* (Cooperative Research Project No. 1932) Columbus, Ohio: The Ohio State University, 1963.

3. ———. "Instruction as Influence Toward Rule-Governed Behavior." *Theories of Instruction.* Edited by James B. Macdonald and Robert R. Leeper. Washington, D. C.: Association for Supervision and Curriculum Development, a department of the National Education Association, 1965.

4. ———. *Model in Theorizing and Research.* Columbus, Ohio: Bureau of Educational Research and Service, The Ohio State University, 1965.

   For a paper on the same topic, see:

   ———. "The Model in Theorizing and Research." (Address given at the International Reading Association Institute V, Use of Theoretical Models in Research, Detroit, May 1965.) *Highlights.* Newark, Delaware: the Association, 1965.

5. ———. *The Study of Education and the Education of Teachers.* (Paper presented at the State University College, Geneseo, N. Y., May 19, 1966.)

6. ———. *The Way of Educational Theorizing.* Columbus, Ohio: Educational Theory Center's Publications, The Ohio State University, May 1966.

Chapter 15. Conclusions and Future Directions

Certain conclusions concerning teacher education emerge from a careful review of the preceding chapters on the research and theoretical work of thirteen outstanding educators. One can conclude quite obviously that there is much data on the topic of teacher education. The works of the thirteen specialists described previously do not represent all of the significant ideas that should find their way into a program for preparing teachers.

However, in terms of the previous discussion in this book, it seems that there is a continued need for more analytic work in the study of teaching. Several descriptions of tools or systems can assist in a careful study of teaching. Perhaps, for those interested in research, some replication of studies is important. Since a number of systems on variables has been described and defined, some work past the descriptive stage can be undertaken. Even though considerable data has been gathered, it might be well to continue basic investigations into what is important in teaching.

For the educator who works directly with prospective teachers, attention should be focused on the teaching act through appropriate analysis, synthesis, and evaluation of ideas. Several writers have identified important variables and strategies developed to the point where immediate use is possible. The teacher educator and his students can: (a) begin to use and test selected logical dimensions in their simulated teaching; (b) define and test certain strategies for cognitive growth; (c) identify, program, and test selected pedagogical moves for teaching; and (d) propose and test ideas on inquiry. Analysis of classroom interaction can be accomplished with a high degree of accuracy after training. Viewing and analyzing the classroom group, school, or school system can place values, goals, and expectations in proper perspective for effective learning and behavioral change. Finally, future teachers, through teaching strategies and concept formation, can begin to develop and design effective units of learning for trial testing and evaluation. The careful search, then, for new methodology and programming of experiences planned to accomplish specified outcomes can be important in teacher education, and the analysis of teaching strategies should receive careful attention from future teachers.

It seems important for those in teacher education to give closer attention to educational goals, within both the affective and cognitive domains, and the meaning they have for the teaching-learning process. A more careful statement of goals, the programming of activities to goal achievement, and the necessary checking of goal attainment can be done with more analytic precision.

This book includes some ideas on using and structuring curriculum experiences in the areas of knowledge and content to provide the future teacher with some guidelines for better teaching. Utilizing these guidelines should foster more effective learning in elementary and secondary school students and in turn provide for more critical work by their teachers. Understanding and using these guidelines must occur at the preservice level.

Sufficient ideas were presented on cognition and concept formation to assist the future teacher in defining necessary dimensions of learning. Careful review of basic concept formation at the preservice level and active participation with elementary or secondary students in applied or simulated situations can help the future teacher to develop the appropriate behavior to carry on this important function. Understanding and experience seem imperative. Also, consideration for higher level thinking should be fostered in the new teacher through a review of parts of this book. Clearly, several important reported studies can assist the teacher educator in his efforts to teach thinking above the knowledge level.

Finally, it would appear both possible and quite necessary for the teacher educator and his students to engage in the creative work of proposing, testing, and evaluating different kinds of selected teaching-learning experiences in a kind of controlled laboratory situation. Novel models and paradigms, as well as established ones, can be tried and checked, promoting more analytic and critical behavior. This kind of active prescribing and testing seems desirous in an inquiry-oriented teacher preparation program.

There appear to be a variety of directions in which the teacher educator can go. He can begin to search for new techniques within the existing framework of a current teacher education program. He can propose something entirely new. Different and exciting things can be planned to develop a more critical teacher in such current courses as "Study of Education," "Introduction to Education," "Methods and Materials for Teaching," and "Foundations of Education." As suggested in Chapter 1, some assumptions must be made, then novel ideas can be developed.

There has been only limited discussion in this book concerning appropriate materials and media necessary to carry out the theoretical and research-based ideas presented. Once the teacher educator understands basic ideas, he has to search for and perhaps create materials and media needed to assist in the development of compatible basic methods or techniques. This is an important function, and one that teacher education students can undertake.

Finally, it seems quite appropriate that interested teacher educators begin to develop completely different teacher preparation patterns. There are sufficient data and ideas present (reported within this book and elsewhere) to encourage such action. An expression of philosophical outcomes and a statement of assumptions are necessary before one begins to state his proposal for a teacher education program. It is to this point that this writer will next address his attention. There appear to be many ideas and materials, reported in this book, for formulating a program which will prepare a more critical and analytical teacher. It is hoped that the reader will draw the same conclusions and begin some creative effort along the same lines.